MUSIC ★ ICONS

LENNON

LUKE CRAMPTON & DAFYDD REES
WITH WELLESLEY MARSH

TASCHEN

HONG KONG KÖLN LONDON LOS ANGELES MADRID PARIS TOKYO

CONTENTS

1

JOHN LENNON: IMAGINE

JOHN LENNON:
IMAGINE

JOHN LENNON :
IMAGINE

JOHN LENNON: IMAGINE

If his legacy were merely that as a founding cornerstone of the Beatles, or as one-half of the most successful song writing team of all time, that would surely be enough to establish his iconic status. But before John Lennon's life was violently cut short at the age of 40, he also forged an immensely popular, vital and varied solo career and pursued a singular vision driven by his singular personality. When the group he co-founded dissolved in 1970, Lennon—perhaps more than any of his former colleagues—reveled in the creative and political freedom suddenly open to him.

An only child, the son of Fred and Julia, John Winston Lennon was born on October 9, 1940 in Woolton, Liverpool, Lancashire. He mostly grew up without his biological parents—his father walked away from the family when John was two, and his free-spirited mother thought it best if the child was instead raised by her sister, Mary Smith and her husband, George. Although Julia would often visit her son, Lennon came to view Aunt Mimi and Uncle George as his immediate family. His teenage years were further perturbed, however, when George died in 1955, and his mother in 1958 (hit by a car). This unorthodox and tragic upbringing would profoundly influence both his character and his music in the decades ahead.

A disenchanted student at Quarry Bank High School and more interested in art and music, Lennon, already a reasonable guitarist, formed a skiffle group, the Quarry Men, with school-mate Pete Shotton at the age of 16. They played at local parties and amateur contests around Liverpool, including a July 6, 1957 gig at St. Peter's Church garden fete where Lennon was first introduced to Paul McCartney.

Despite a poor academic record Lennon still managed to enroll at the Liverpool College of Art in 1957. Though his love of art would remain throughout his life, it was his musical career alongside his Liverpudlian chums which increasingly dominated his time and creative energy. His friendship, musical partnership and shared ambition with McCartney steered the pair through an apprenticeship in the Quarry Men, soon joined by George Harrison, which evolved into the Silver Beetles before becoming the Beatles, with Ringo Starr rounding out the Fab Four.

By the time the magical sixties decade of the Beatles was over, the world had witnessed an unmatched sonic union of four unique musical talents and personalities—their success underpinned by the perfect symmetry of countless and timeless Lennon and McCartney compositions. Theirs became the most popular song-writing unit of all time, propelling the band's fortunes to a rarified height as the most successful recording group ever. Both truly gifted songsmiths, vocalists and musicians, it was arguably Lennon who most assertively pushed the creative boundaries of the group after its initial pop success.

During the Beatles slow self-destruction at the end of the decade, Lennon had become a restless spirit, keen to develop beyond the confines of being in the world's most popular band. Utterly smitten upon meeting 33-year old Japanese artiste, Yoko Ono in 1966, the pair released two avant-garde albums before the Beatles' dissolution, though it was his 1969 hit, *Give Peace A Chance*, which established his most accessible solo credentials. Together with *Imagine*, this would become his most identifiable solo platform: using the skill of his song writing and performance genius to distill a universal message of world peace. The earliest years of Lennon's solo flight best synthesized this idealistic vision: during a three-year span (1969–1972), Lennon wrote and recorded three simple peace anthems: *Give Peace A Chance*, *Happy Xmas (War Is Over)* and the evergreen classic, *Imagine*—each of which would prove to be his most enduring solo songs.

Relocating to New York in August 1971 he would remain on American soil until his death, comfortable and devoted to Yoko but hemmed in by increasingly hostile immigration authorities and a neurotic Nixon administration which was troubled by Lennon's outspoken activism. Seemingly inseparable in art, music, life and ideology, John and Yoko were endlessly creative in their attempts to use the media to spread their message of love.

Lennon recorded one album per year from 1970–1975, building an ever-inventive and commercially successful catalog, yielding 10 United States hit singles and popular collaborations with the likes of Elton John and David Bowie. Reunited after a 16-month split, Lennon elected to take on the role of househusband, beginning a five-year sabbatical raising their only child, Sean.

Starting over in 1980 to record his first album in five years, and seemingly more at peace with himself than ever, Lennon's senseless murder at the end of that year shook the world. It was unimaginable. While his widow has continued to keep his cause and ideals alive, it is Lennon's music—both as a Beatle and as a solo artist—which continues to inspire and move music lovers around the globe.

Singer, composer, guitarist, pianist, poet, actor, artist, peace activist, provocateur, renaissance man—all in 40 years. Posthumously inducted into the Songwriters Hall of Fame in 1987, and the Rock and Roll Hall of Fame in 1994, Lennon's legacy survives not only as a musical icon, but also as a lasting symbol of a simple idea: a brotherhood of man.

JOHN LENNON: IMAGINE

John Lennons Karriere als Mitbegründer der Beatles oder als eine Hälfte des erfolgreichsten Songwriter-Teams aller Zeiten hätte sicherlich gereicht, um ihm seinen Status als Kultfigur zu sichern. Doch bevor John Lennons Leben mit nur 40 Jahren ein gewaltsames Ende fand, gelang ihm außerdem noch eine Solokarriere als ungemein populärer, vitaler, vielseitiger und einzigartiger Künstler mit einer großen Vision. Als die Band, die er mitbegründet hatte, sich 1970 auflöste, genoss Lennon vielleicht mehr noch als die anderen Bandmitglieder die neue kreative und politische Freiheit, die sich ihm plötzlich bot.

John Winston Lennon kam als einziges Kind von Fred und Julia Lennon am 9. Oktober 1940 in Woolton, Liverpool, auf die Welt. Er wuchs weitgehend ohne seine leiblichen Eltern auf – sein Vater verließ die Familie, als John zwei war, und seine Mutter hielt es in ihrer unkonventionellen Einstellung für das Beste, ihn von ihrer Schwester Mary Smith und deren Mann George aufziehen zu lassen. Julia Lennon besuchte ihren Sohn zwar häufig, doch John betrachtete Tante Mimi und Onkel George als seine eigentliche Familie. Einen tiefen Einschnitt erlebte er als Teenager, als George 1955 starb und seine Mutter 1958 bei einem Autounfall ums Leben kam. John Lennons ungewöhnliche und tragische Kindheit und Jugend prägten seinen Charakter und seine Musik für Jahrzehnte.

Als Schüler an der Quarry Bank High School war John desillusioniert und interessierte sich eigentlich nur für Kunst und Musik. Im Alter von 16 Jahren konnte er bereits recht gut Gitarre spielen und gründete zusammen mit seinem Schulkameraden Pete Shotton eine Skiffleband, The Quarry Men. Sie spielten im Raum Liverpool auf Partys und bei Wettbewerben, so auch am 6. Juli 1957 bei einem Gartenfest der Gemeinde St. Peter, wo John Paul McCartney kennenlernte.

Trotz seines schlechten Notendurchschnitts schaffte John Lennon es, 1957 einen Studienplatz am Liverpool College of Art zu ergattern. Seine Liebe zur bildenden Kunst blieb ihm zwar ein Leben lang erhalten, aber es war seine musikalische Karriere mit den Jungs aus Liverpool, die seine Zeit und kreative Energie immer stärker in Anspruch nahm. Paul McCartney und ihn verband eine große Freundschaft und gemeinsamer Ehrgeiz, und sie übten ihre musikalische Zusammenarbeit bei den Quarry Men ein, zu denen sich bald auch George Harrison gesellte. Sie entwickelten sich weiter zu den Silver Beetles, aus denen schließlich The Beatles wurden, als Ringo Starr dazu kam und die „Fab Four" komplett waren.

Am Ende jenes magischen Jahrzehnts der Beatles, der 1960er Jahre, war die Welt Zeuge einer einmaligen Verschmelzung vier beispielloser musikalischer Talente und Persönlichkeiten geworden. Den Grundstein für den unglaublichen Erfolg der Beatles legten Lennon und McCartney mit der perfekten Symmetrie ihrer zahllosen, zeitlosen Kompositionen. Die beiden bildeten das populärste kompositorische Zweigespann aller Zeiten und eroberten mit ihrer Band den Rang als erfolgreichste Musikgruppe aller Zeiten. Beide waren hochbegabte Wortschmiede, Komponisten, Sänger und Musiker. Doch es war John Lennon, der sich nach dem anfänglichen Erfolg der Band in der Popmusik am nachdrücklichsten für eine kreative Ausdehnung der musikalischen Möglichkeiten einsetzte.

Als er 1966 die 33-jährige japanische Künstlerin Yoko Ono kennenlernte, war er vollkommen fasziniert von ihr und brachte schon vor Auflösung der Beatles zwei Avantgarde-Alben mit ihr zusammen heraus. Doch es war sein Solohit von 1969, *Give Peace A Chance*, der auch seine Musik als Solokünstler einem breiten Publikum zugänglich machte. Dieser Song bildete zusammen mit *Imagine* das, was man als Zentrum seiner Solokarriere bezeichnen kann: Er setzte seine Fähigkeiten als Komponist und Musiker ein, um eine allgemeinverständliche Botschaft zu vermitteln – den Wunsch nach Weltfrieden.

Im August 1971 zog John Lennon nach New York und blieb bis zu seinem Tod in Amerika, wo er eine glückliche, hingebungsvolle Beziehung mit Yoko Ono führte, aber zunehmend von der feindseligen amerikanischen Einwanderungsbehörde bedrängt wurde: Die neurotische Nixon-Regierung, der John Lennons Aktivismus gegen den Strich ging, machte ihm das Leben schwer. John und Yoko schienen in Kunst, Musik, Liebe und Ideologie unzertrennlich und fanden immer neue Wege, die Medien zu nutzen, um ihre Botschaft der Liebe zu verbreiten.

Zwischen 1970 und 1975 nahm John Lennon jedes Jahr ein neues Album auf, eines fantasievoller und erfolgreicher als das andere. Dabei entstanden zehn US-Hitsingles und zahlreiche erfolgreiche Aufnahmen in Zusammenarbeiten mit Musikern wie Elton John und David Bowie. Nachdem sie sich für sechzehn Monate getrennt hatten, fand das Paar 1975 wieder zusammen. John Lennon wurde hauptberuflicher Vater und hielt sich fünf Jahre lang vom Aufnahmestudio und vom Rampenlicht fern, um sich in ihrer New Yorker Wohnung ganz seinem Sohn Sean widmen zu können.

1980 kehrte er ins Plattenstudio zurück, nahm sein erstes Album seit fünf Jahren auf und wirkte im Einklang mit sich selbst wie nie zuvor. Seine Ermordung am Ende des gleichen Jahres erschütterte die ganze Welt. Sein Tod war ein unfassbarer Schlag. Seine Ideale und Überzeugungen werden von seiner Witwe hochgehalten, aber es ist vor allem seine Musik – sowohl mit den Beatles als auch als Solomusiker –, von der Menschen in aller Welt nach wie vor inspiriert und berührt werden.

In seiner kurzen Lebenszeit wirkte er als Sänger, Komponist, Gitarrist, Pianist, Dichter, Schauspieler, Künstler, Friedensaktivist, Provokateur und Mann der Welt. Posthum wurde er 1987 in die Songwriters Hall of Fame aufgenommen, 1994 in die Rock and Roll Hall of Fame. John Lennons Vermächtnis ist nicht nur das einer musikalischen Ikone, sondern auch Ausdruck einer einfachen Überzeugung: Alle Menschen sind Brüder und Schwestern.

JOHN LENNON : IMAGINE

Même s'il n'était resté que l'un des cofondateurs et des piliers des Beatles, ou la moitié du tandem auteur-compositeur le plus brillant de tous les temps, il aurait mérité son statut d'idole. Mais avant que la vie de John Lennon soit fauchée, à tout juste 40 ans, il s'est également construit une carrière solo immensément populaire, vivace et variée, en suivant la voie singulière que lui indiquait sa personnalité singulière. Lorsque le groupe qu'il a créé s'est séparé, en 1970, Lennon a pu goûter – sans doute davantage qu'aucun de ses trois anciens collègues – à la liberté créative et politique qui s'offrait à lui.

Fils unique de Fred et Julia, John Winston Lennon naît le 9 octobre 1940 dans le quartier de Woolton, à Liverpool (Lancashire). Il grandit sans ses parents biologiques, ou presque – son père quitte la famille quand John a deux ans et sa mère, à l'esprit indépendant, préfère que l'enfant soit élevé par sa sœur Mary Smith et son mari George. Julia rend souvent visite à son fils, mais Lennon considère rapidement tante Mimi et oncle George comme sa vraie famille. Son adolescence est encore davantage perturbée par la mort de George, en 1955, puis celle de sa mère (renversée par une voiture) trois ans plus tard. Cette enfance peu orthodoxe et tragique marque profondément sa personnalité et sa musique.

Lycéen désenchanté de la Quarry Bank High School, davantage intéressé par l'art et la musique que par les études, Lennon, déjà bon guitariste, forme un groupe de skiffle, les Quarry Men, avec son camarade de classe Pete Shotton. Il a 16 ans. Les deux garçons se produisent à l'occasion de fêtes locales et participent à des concours d'amateurs à Liverpool. Le 6 juillet 1957, ils jouent à la fête de l'église St. Peter, où Lennon fait la connaissance de Paul McCartney.

Malgré un passé scolaire médiocre, Lennon parvient à s'inscrire au Liverpool College of Art en 1957 (son amour de l'art perdurera tout au long de sa vie). Il consacre cependant l'essentiel de son temps et de son énergie à la carrière musicale qu'il mène avec ses copains parallèlement à ses études. Unis par l'amitié, la complicité musicale et une même ambition, Paul McCartney et Lennon font leur apprentissage sous la bannière des Quarry Men ; rejoints par George Harrison, ils deviennent les Silver Beetles avant de se rebaptiser Beatles lorsque Ringo Starr vient parfaire le fameux « Fab Four ».

Le monde sort de la décennie magique des Beatles (les années 1960) enrichi de cette rencontre de quatre personnages et talents musicaux hors du commun, dont le succès s'appuie sur la symétrie parfaite des compositions innombrables et intemporelles de Lennon et McCartney. Leurs chansons, parmi les plus célèbres de tous les temps, ont propulsé le groupe jusqu'à des sommets commerciaux et populaires jamais atteints auparavant. Si les deux hommes étaient des paroliers, des compositeurs, des chanteurs et des musiciens très doués, c'est sans doute Lennon qui a élargi l'horizon créatif du groupe de la façon la plus active et décomplexée après son succès initial sous l'étiquette « pop ».

Pendant la lente autodestruction des Beatles, à la fin des années 1960, Lennon est un esprit agité, impatient de prendre son essor au-delà des limites imposées par leur statut de plus célèbre groupe du monde. En 1966, il tombe éperdument amoureux de l'artiste japonaise de 33 ans Yoko Ono ; le couple sort deux albums d'avant-garde avant la dissolution des Beatles, mais c'est son tube pacifiste de 1969, *Give Peace A Chance* qui consacre sa carrière en solo. Avec ce titre très accessible et *Imagine*, il met ses talents de compositeur et son génie de la performance au service d'un message universel de paix. Les premières années de Lennon sans les Beatles sont celles qui synthétisent le mieux sa vision idéaliste : en trois ans (1969-1972), Lennon écrit et enregistre trois hymnes simples à la paix dans le monde – *Give Peace A Chance*, *Happy Xmas (War Is Over)* et le grand classique, *Imagine* – qui s'imprimeront dans les mémoires de plusieurs générations successives.

En août 1971, Lennon s'installe à New York. Il restera sur le sol américain jusqu'à sa mort, aux côté de Yoko, dans le confort matériel et affectif, malgré l'hostilité croissante des services d'immigration et de l'administration Nixon, agacée par son militantisme sans détour. Inséparables dans l'art, la musique, la vie et l'idéologie, John et Yoko se dévouent sincèrement à la cause de la révolution pacifique et recourent à leur créativité débordante pour attirer l'attention des médias et diffuser leur message d'amour.

Lennon enregistre un album par an entre 1970 et 1975, étoffant une œuvre inventive qui rencontre aussi le succès commercial : dix chansons entrent dans les dix meilleures ventes de 45 tours aux États-Unis et il collabore avec des personnalités de premier plan comme Elton John ou David Bowie. De nouveau aux côtés de Yoko après une trêve de 16 mois, Lennon choisit de se vouer à son rôle d'époux et de père. Il passe cinq années loin des projecteurs et des studios pour élever son fils unique dans leur appartement de New York.

Lorsqu'il retrouve les studios d'enregistrement en 1980, il semble plus en paix avec lui-même que jamais auparavant et son assassinat absurde, à la fin de cette année, bouleverse le monde entier. Un acte inimaginable. Si sa veuve perpétue son combat et ses idéaux, c'est la musique de Lennon – à la fois en tant que Beatle qu'en solo – qui continue à inspirer et émouvoir les passionnés de musique à travers le monde.

Chanteur, compositeur, guitariste, pianiste, poète, acteur, artiste, militant pacifiste, provocateur, « homme universel », tout cela en 40 ans. Inscrit à titre posthume au Songwriters Hall of Fame en 1987 et au Rock and Roll Hall of Fame en 1994, Lennon demeure non seulement une icône de la musique, mais aussi le symbole indéfectible d'une idée simple : la communion entre les hommes.

hneider

2

CHRONOLOGY

CHRONOLOGIE

CHRONOLOGIE

WITH THE BEATLES

MIT DEN BEATLES

AVEC LES BEATLES

SATURDAY JULY 6, 1957

The Quarry Men Skiffle Group perform at the St. Peter's Parish Church Garden Fête in the Liverpool district of Woolton, when bassist Ivan Vaughan introduces the group's lead singer, 16-year old John Lennon, to another local musician, 15-year old Paul McCartney at the close of the band's set. Impressed with McCartney's knowledge of rock 'n' roll lyrics of the day and his ability to tune a guitar, Lennon invites him to join the group. So begins a friendship and songwriting partnership which will evolve into the formation of the Beatles.

Die Skiffleband The Quarry Men spielt beim Gartenfest der Kirchengemeinde St. Peter im Liverpooler Stadtteil Woolton. Bassist Ivan Vaughan macht den Sänger der Gruppe, den 16-jährigen John Lennon, nach dem Auftritt mit dem 15-jährigen Paul McCartney bekannt. John ist beeindruckt, wie gut Paul sich mit Rock 'n' Roll-Texten auskennt und wie gut er Gitarre spielt, und fordert ihn auf, der Band beizutreten. So beginnt die Freundschaft und Zusammenarbeit der beiden Songschreiber, aus der sich später die Beatles entwickeln.

Le Quarry Men Skiffle Group participe à la fête de la paroisse St. Peter, à Liverpool, dans le quartier de Woolton ; à la fin du concert, le bassiste, Ivan Vaughan, présente le chanteur du groupe, John Lennon, âgé de 16 ans, à un autre musicien de la scène locale, Paul McCartney, 15 ans. Impressionné par la culture musicale de McCartney, qui connaît les paroles de la plupart des tubes rock 'n' roll du moment et sait jouer de la guitare, Lennon lui propose de se joindre au groupe. Ainsi commence une amitié et une collaboration artistique qui conduit à la formation des Beatles.

WEDNESDAY, AUGUST 17, 1960

Lennon and his fellow Beatles play their first date in West Germany, at the Indra Club in Hamburg. They will perform through the end of November, returning in April next year and the year after.

John Lennon und die Beatles haben ihr erstes Konzert-Engagement in Deutschland, im Indra Club in Hamburg. Dort treten sie bis Ende November täglich auf und kehren auch im April des Folgejahrs und im Jahr danach nach Hamburg zurück.

Lennon et ses amis Beatles jouent leur premier concert en Allemagne, à l'Indra Club de Hambourg. Ils tournent jusqu'à fin novembre et y reviendront en avril de l'année suivante, puis encore l'année d'après.

© Rock and Roll Hall of Fame

THURSDAY, FEBRUARY 9, 1961

The Beatles make their Cavern Club debut in Liverpool, the first of many popular lunchtime gigs. They are paid £5.

The Beatles haben ihren ersten Auftritt im Cavern Club in Liverpool, den ersten von vielen, damals beliebten Gigs zur Mittagszeit. Ihr Honorar beträgt fünf Pfund.

Les Beatles font leurs débuts britanniques au Cavern Club de Liverpool, à l'heure du déjeuner. Ils sont payés 5 livres pour ces concerts légendaires.

MONDAY, JUNE 4, 1962

Having been given a Beatles demo tape by band manager, Brian Epstein, EMI/Parlophone A&R head George Martin signs the group to a provisional recording contract. The quartet will make its first visit to Abbey Road Studios in St. John's Wood, London in two days time, a session at which they record three Lennon/McCartney originals.

Der Manager der Band, Brian Epstein, hat dem A&R-Chef von EMI/Parlophone George Martin ein Demoband der Beatles in die Hand gedrückt, woraufhin er ihnen einen provisorischen Plattenvertrag vorlegt. Zwei Tage später besucht das Quartett zum ersten Mal die Abbey Road Studios in St. John's Wood, London; bei der Session werden drei Stücke von Lennon/McCartney aufgenommen.

Après avoir reçu une bande démo des Beatles envoyée par leur manager Brian Epstein, le patron d'EMI/Parlophone George Martin signe avec le groupe un contrat d'enregistrement. Deux jours plus tard, les Beatles entrent pour la première fois dans les studios londoniens d'Abbey Road, à St. John's Wood. Ils enregistrent trois compositions du duo Lennon/McCartney.

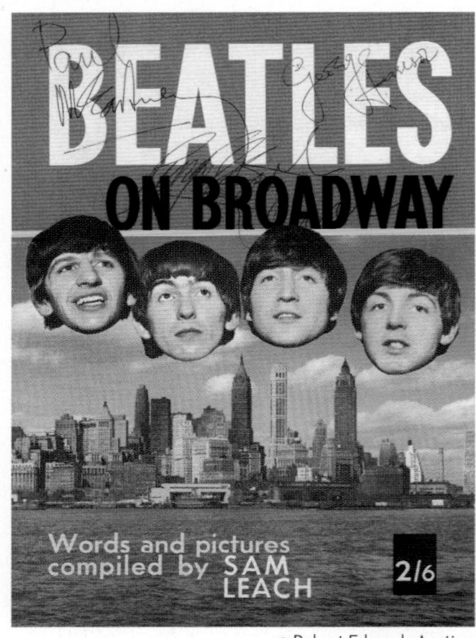

© Robert Edwards Auction

"They were pretty awful. I understand why other record companies turned them down ... but when I met them, I liked them."

„Sie waren ziemlich schlecht. Mir wurde klar, warum sie von anderen Plattenfirmen abgelehnt worden waren ... aber als ich sie kennenlernte, mochte ich sie sofort."

« Ils étaient plutôt mauvais. Je comprends pourquoi d'autres maisons de disques les ont refusés... Mais quand je les ai rencontrés, ils m'ont plu. »

GEORGE MARTIN

SUNDAY, FEBRUARY 9, 1964

With Beatlemania having taken off in their home country the previous year, the group makes its live United States debut on CBS-TV's "The Ed Sullivan Show," a national cultural event watched by an estimated 73 million viewers. For an appearance fee of $2,400 they perform *All My Loving, Till There Was You, She Loves You, I Saw Her Standing There* and *I Want To Hold Your Hand*. With Lennon and McCartney at the helm as principal songwriters and vocalists, the Beatles will dominate the decade worldwide like no other music act before or since—though their entire EMI recording career will span only seven years.

Die Beatlemania hat ihr Heimatland bereits im Vorjahr überrollt – jetzt treten die Beatles zum ersten Mal live in den USA auf, bei der CBS-Sendung „The Ed Sullivan Show", ein landesweites Ereignis, das ca. 73 Mio. Zuschauer am Bildschirm verfolgen. Für eine Gage von 2.400 US-Dollar spielen sie *All My Loving, Till There Was You, She Loves You, I Saw Her Standing There* und *I Want To Hold Your Hand*. Mit den führenden Köpfen John Lennon und Paul McCartney als Sänger und Songwriter sind die Beatles weltweit zehn Jahre lang so erfolgreich wie keine andere Band vor oder nach ihnen – dabei nehmen sie insgesamt nur sieben Jahr lang für EMI Schallplatten auf.

Alors que la « Beatlemania » bat son plein dans leur pays natal, le groupe part à la conquête des États-Unis. Il fait ses débuts dans la fameuse émission « The Ed Sullivan Show », sur CBS, suivie par quelques 73 millions de téléspectateurs. Pour un cachet de 2 400 dollars, ils jouent *All My Loving, Till There Was You, She Loves You, I Saw Her Standing There* et *I Want To Hold Your Hand*. Avec Lennon et McCartney comme têtes pensantes et compositeurs de la plupart des titres, les Beatles dominent la décennie musicale dans le monde entier, comme aucun autre groupe n'y est parvenu ni avant ni depuis, alors que leur carrière discographique chez EMI ne durera que sept ans.

THURSDAY, APRIL 23, 1964

On the occasion of William Shakespeare's 400th birth, John Lennon is guest of honor at a Foyle's Literary Lunch at the Dorchester Hotel. His book of nonsense verse and rhyme, **In His Own Write**, wins the Foyle's Literary Prize. Accepting the award, the usually verbose Lennon merely says: "Thank you very much. You've got a lucky face."

Bei einer Feier zum 400. Geburtstag von William Shakespeare ist John Lennon Ehrengast bei Foyle's Literary Lunch im Dorchester Hotel. Sein Buch mit Reimen und Nonsensversen **In His Own Write** gewinnt den Foyle's Literary Prize. Bei Entgegennahme des Preises sagt der sonst so redegewandte John Lennon nur: „Vielen Dank. Sie haben ein Glücksgesicht."

À l'occasion du 400e anniversaire de William Shakespeare, John Lennon est l'invité d'honneur du Foyle's Literary Lunch, au Dorchester Hotel. Son livre **En flagrant délire** (**In His Own Write**), qui mêle versification et écriture automatique, reçoit le prix Foyle, et John Lennon, habituellement volubile, l'accueille par cette formule laconique : « Merci beaucoup. Vous m'avez l'air chanceux. »

THURSDAY, AUGUST 11, 1966

Two weeks after American **Datebook** magazine has reproduced a March 4 Lennon interview by Maureen Cleave in London's **Evening Standard** newspaper—in which Lennon proclaimed that the Beatles are "more popular than Jesus now"—the three United States television networks broadcast the group's press conference from the Astor Towers Hotel in Chicago. Lennon publicly apologizes for his controversial remarks which have resulted in several American radio stations permanently banning Beatles music, and mass burnings of Beatles records and memorabilia. Thurman H. Babbs, the pastor of the New Haven Baptist Church in Cleveland, will vow to excommunicate any parishioner who goes to a Beatles' concert or listens to their music.

Zwei Wochen nachdem die amerikanische Zeitschrift **Datebook** ein Interview nachgedruckt hat, das John Lennon am 4. März mit Maureen Cleave von der Londoner Zeitung **Evening Standard** geführt hat – John hatte darin behauptet, die Beatles seien „jetzt populärer als Jesus" – übertragen die drei großen amerikanischen Fernsehsender die Pressekonferenz der Band im Astor Towers Hotel in Chicago. John entschuldigt sich öffentlich für seine umstrittene Äußerung, die dazu geführt hat, dass viele amerikanische Radiosender alle Beatles-Musik aus ihrem Programm verbannt haben und Beatles-Platten und -Souvenirs massenhaft verbrannt wurden. Thurman H. Babbs, Pfarrer der New Haven Baptist Church in Cleveland, schwört, jedes Gemeindemitglied zu exkommunizieren, das zu einem Beatles-Konzert geht oder ihre Musik hört.

Deux semaines après la reprise dans le magazine américain **Datebook** de l'interview de Lennon par Maureen Cleave parue le 4 mars dans l'**Evening Standard** de Londres – dans laquelle Lennon affirme que les Beatles sont « plus populaires que Jésus » –, les trois chaînes de télévision américaines diffusent la conférence de presse donnée par le groupe à l'Astor Towers Hotel de Chicago. Lennon fait des excuses publiques pour ses remarques polémiques, qui ont eu des conséquences spectaculaires : plusieurs stations de radio ont annoncé qu'elles ne diffuseraient plus jamais de chansons des Beatles et des centaines d'Américains ont brûlé des disques du groupe, ainsi que d'autres objets à son effigie. Thurman H. Babbs, pasteur de l'église baptiste New Haven de Cleveland, promet qu'il excommuniera tout paroissien qui se rendrait à un concert des Beatles ou écouterait leur musique.

"If I had said television is more popular than Jesus, I might have got away with it, but I just happened to be talking to a friend and I used the words 'Beatles' as a remote thing, not as what I think—as Beatles, as those other Beatles like other people see us. I just said 'they' are having more influence on kids and things than anything else, including Jesus."

„Hätte ich behauptet, das Fernsehen sei populärer als Jesus, wäre ich vielleicht damit durchgekommen. Ich habe nur bei einem Gespräch mit Freunden die Beatles im weitesten Sinne als beliebigen Vergleich angeführt. Nicht, wie ich die Beatles sehe, sondern wie andere sie sehen. Ich meinte nur, dass ‚sie' die Jugend insgesamt mehr beeinflussen als alles andere, inklusive Jesus."

« Si j'avais dit que la télévision était plus populaire que Jésus, je m'en serais peut-être tiré, mais il se trouve que je parlais à une amie et que j'ai employé le mot "Beatles" pour désigner une image, pas ce que nous sommes en tant que personnes, mais les Beatles comme les autres nous voient. J'ai simplement dit qu'"eux" avaient plus d'influence sur les gosses que n'importe quoi d'autre, y compris Jésus. »

JOHN LENNON, AUGUST 11, 1966

1526

TUESDAY, SEPTEMBER 6, 1966

Having flown to Celle, West Germany, yesterday to begin work on the Richard Lester-directed film "How I Won The War" in the role of Private Gripweed, Lennon has a very public short-back-and-sides haircut from Klaus Baruck at the Inn On The Heath.

John Lennon ist am Vortag nach Celle zu den Dreharbeiten des Richard-Lester-Films „Wie ich den Krieg gewann" geflogen, in dem er die Rolle des Soldaten Gripweed spielt. Er lässt sich in einer öffentlichen Aktion die Haare von Klaus Baruck im Inn On The Heath kurz schneiden.

Arrivé la veille à Celle (Allemagne de l'Ouest), pour participer au film de Richard Lester « Comment j'ai gagné la guerre », dans lequel il joue le deuxième classe Gripweed, Lennon passe sous la tondeuse de Klaus Baruck, qui lui fait la coupe réglementaire « nuque et tempes courtes » devant la presse, dans les salons du Inn On The Heath.

WEDNESDAY, NOVEMBER 9, 1966

Two days after returning from filming in Spain, Lennon meets 33-year-old Japanese conceptual artiste Yoko Ono for the first time, at a private preview for Ono's avant-garde "Unfinished Paintings And Objects" exhibition at the Indica Gallery in Mason's Yard, London. Ono helped found the Fluxus movement in New York with George Macuinas.

Zwei Tage nach der Rückkehr von Dreharbeiten in Spanien lernt John Lennon die 33-jährige japanische Konzeptkünstlerin Yoko Ono bei einer privaten Vorbesichtigung von Yokos avantgardistischer Ausstellung „Unfinished Paintings And Objects" in der Indica Gallery in Mason's Yard in London kennen. Yoko Ono war zusammen mit George Macuinas eine der Begründerinnen der Fluxus-Bewegung in New York.

Deux jours après son retour de tournage en Espagne, Lennon rencontre Yoko Ono, artiste conceptuelle japonaise de 33 ans, lors d'un vernissage de son exposition d'avant-garde « Unfinished Paintings And Objects », à la galerie londonienne Indica. Ono a notamment participé à la création du mouvement Fluxus, à New York, avec George Macuinas.

THURSDAY, NOVEMBER 24, 1966

The Beatles begin work on a new Lennon composition, *Strawberry Fields Forever* as they return to Abbey Road, to begin work on ***Sgt. Pepper's Lonely Hearts Club Band***, although the song will not appear on the album. With Lennon and McCartney increasingly writing solo (though their songs are still formally co-credited), *Strawberry Fields* is named after a Salvation Army house on Beaconsfield Road in Liverpool where Lennon played as a child.

Die Beatles fangen mit der Arbeit an einer neuen Lennon-Komposition an: *Strawberry Fields Forever*. Sie kehren ins Plattenstudio in der Abbey Road zurück und beginnen mit Aufnahmen zu ***Sgt. Pepper's Lonely Hearts Club Band***, dieses Stück wird dann allerdings später nicht auf dem Album veröffentlicht. John und Paul schreiben ihre Songs immer öfter allein (auch wenn formell nach wie vor stets beide als Komponisten genannt werden). *Strawberry Fields* ist der Name eines Hauses der Heilsarmee an der Beaconsfield Road in Liverpool, wo John als Kind oft gespielt hat.

Les Beatles commencent à travailler sur une nouvelle composition de Lennon, *Strawberry Fields Forever*, et retournent à Abbey Road pour débuter l'enregistrement de ***Sgt. Pepper's Lonely Hearts Club Band***; la chanson ne figurera toutefois pas sur cet album. Lennon et McCartney multiplient les compositions personnelles (même si les chansons sont toujours créditées à l'ensemble du groupe). Le nom *Strawberry Fields* vient du foyer de l'Armée du Salut de Liverpool où Lennon allait jouer quand il était enfant.

SUNDAY, NOVEMBER 27, 1966

Lennon films a sketch for a forthcoming edition of British satire actors Peter Cook and Dudley Moore's BBC2-TV show "Not Only ... But Also." He plays a nightclub doorman outside a Gentlemen's toilet in Broadwick Street. The show will air on December 26.

John Lennon filmt einen Sketch für die nächste Ausgabe der BBC2-Fernsehserie „Not Only ... But Also" der britischen Komiker Peter Cook und Dudley Moore. Er spielt den Türsteher eines Nachtclubs, der vor einer Herrentoilette auf der Broadwick Street steht. Die Folge wird am 26. Dezember ausgestrahlt.

Lennon filme un sketch pour la prochaine édition de l'émission satirique britannique présentée par Peter Cook et Dudley Moore sur la BBC2, « Not Only ... But Also ». Il joue un videur de boîte de nuit attendant devant des sanisettes pour messieurs sur Broadwick Street. L'émission est diffusée le 26 décembre.

SUNDAY, MAY 19, 1968

Some seven months after anonymously sponsoring Yoko Ono's "Half A Wind" exhibition at the Lisson Art Gallery, Lennon invites her to Kenwood, his house in Weybridge, Surrey. As the evening unfolds they record material that will emerge as the album ***Two Virgins***. As the sun rises, they consummate their relationship. Later in the day, Lennon's wife Cynthia (whom he married in July 1962) returns from a vacation in Greece to discover her husband's latest infidelity.

Sieben Monate nachdem er anonym Yoko Onos Ausstellung „Half A Wind" in der Lisson Art Gallery als Sponsor unterstützt hat, lädt John Lennon sie in sein Haus Kenwood in Weybridge, Surrey, ein. Im Laufe der Nacht nehmen sie Material auf, aus dem später das Album ***Two Virgins*** wird. Als die Sonne aufgeht, werden sie ein Paar. Später am selben Tag kehrt Johns Frau Cynthia (die er im Juli 1962 geheiratet hatte) von einem Griechenlandurlaub zurück und wird mit dem neusten Seitensprung ihres Mannes konfrontiert.

Environ sept mois après avoir financé anonymement l'exposition de Yoko Ono « Half A Wind » à la Lisson Art Gallery, Lennon l'invite à Kenwood, sa maison de Weybridge, dans le Surrey. Au cours de la soirée, ils enregistrent ce qui deviendra l'album ***Two Virgins***. Lorsque le soleil se lève, ils consomment leur union. Quelques heures plus tard, la femme de Lennon, Cynthia (qu'il a épousée en juillet 1962) revient de vacances en Grèce et découvre brutalement la dernière infidélité de son mari.

THURSDAY, MAY 30, 1968

Utterly smitten with his new love, John brings Yoko to a Beatles session at Abbey Road for the first time, as the group begins work on a new Lennon song, *Revolution*.

John Lennon will seine neue Geliebte immer um sich haben und bringt Yoko zum ersten Mal zu einer Beatles-Session in der Abbey Road mit. Dort beginnen die Aufnahmen zu einem neuen Lennon-Song: *Revolution*.

Follement épris de la nouvelle femme de sa vie, John amène Yoko à une séance d'enregistrement à Abbey Road pour la première fois, alors que le groupe commence à travailler sur la dernière chanson de Lennon, *Revolution*.

TUESDAY, JUNE 18, 1968

Three days after planting two acorns at a "happening" as part of the National Sculpture Exhibition in the grounds of Coventry Cathedral, John and Yoko attend the opening night of his one-act play "The Lennon Play: In His Own Write," based on his two books **In His Own Write** and **A Spaniard In The Works**, at the Old Vic—the home of the National Theatre. The play is directed by Victor Spinetti, who appeared in both "A Hard Day's Night" and "Help!"

Drei Tage nachdem sie bei einem „Happening" im Rahmen der National Sculpture Exhibition auf dem Gelände der Coventry Cathedral zwei Eicheln eingepflanzt haben, sehen John und Yoko sich die Premiere seines Einakters „The Lennon Play: In His Own Write" an, der auf seinen beiden Büchern **In His Own Write** und **A Spaniard In The Works** basiert. Das Stück wird im Old Vic gezeigt, Heimat des englischen Nationaltheaters, Regie führt Victor Spinetti, der auch in „A Hard Day's Night" und „Help!" zu sehen war.

Trois jours après avoir planté deux glands sur les terres de la cathédrale de Coventry pour un happening organisé dans le cadre de la National Sculpture Exhibition, John et Yoko assistent à la première représentation de sa pièce en un acte, « The Lennon Play : In His Own Write, » basée sur ses deux livres (**En flagrant délire** et **A Spaniard In The Works**), à l'Old Vic – siège du National Theatre. La pièce est mise en scène par Victor Spinetti, qui apparaît dans « A Hard Day's Night » et « Help! »

MONDAY, JULY 1, 1968

Lennon celebrates the opening of his own exhibition "You Are Here" at the Robert Fraser Gallery in Duke Street, London, by releasing 365 helium balloons.

John feiert die Vernissage seiner Ausstellung „You Are Here" in der Robert Fraser Gallery in der Duke Street in London und lässt 365 Heliumballons fliegen.

Lennon célèbre le vernissage de son exposition « You Are Here » à la galerie Robert Fraser de Duke Street, à Londres, par un lâcher de 365 ballons gonflés à l'hélium.

SATURDAY, AUGUST 24, 1968

Two days after Cynthia Lennon files for divorce on the grounds of adultery, John and Yoko appear on London Weekend Television's "Frost On Sunday." (Two weeks later, the Beatles premiere *Hey Jude* on the same show.)

Zwei Tage nachdem Cynthia Lennon die Scheidung wegen Ehebruchs eingereicht hat, treten John und Yoko zusammen in der Sendung „Frost On Sunday" im London Weekend Television auf. (Zwei Wochen später spielen die Beatles in derselben Sendung zum ersten Mal *Hey Jude*.)

Cynthia Lennon a demandé le divorce deux jours plus tôt pour adultère, et John et Yoko participent à l'émission « Frost On Sunday » sur la chaîne London Weekend Television (Deux semaines plus tard, les Beatles présenteront *Hey Jude* dans la même émission.)

SATURDAY, OCTOBER 19, 1968

Taken to Paddington Green police station yesterday after cannabis is discovered in Ringo Starr's apartment in Montagu Square in London, where they are staying, Lennon and Ono are remanded on bail at Marylebone Magistrates' Court and charged with possession of cannabis and obstructing police in the execution of a search warrant. Lennon will plead guilty to cannabis possession and will be fined £150 with 20 guineas costs. Yoko will be cleared. The arresting officer, Detective Sergeant Norman Pilcher, will subsequently be imprisoned for planting evidence in several other cases.

In Ringo Starrs Apartment am Montagu Square in London, wo John und Yoko wohnen, wird Cannabis entdeckt. Die beiden werden auf die Polizeiwache Paddington Green gebracht, in Untersuchungshaft festgehalten und vor dem Marylebone Magistrates' Court des Cannabisbesitzes und der Behinderung der Polizei bei der Durchführung einer Hausdurchsuchung angeklagt. John bekennt sich des Cannabisbesitzes für schuldig und erhält eine Geldstrafe von 150 Pfund, Yoko wird freigesprochen. Der Polizist, der die beiden festgenommen hat, Detective Sergeant Norman Pilcher, muss später selbst ins Gefängnis, weil er in mehreren anderen Fällen falsche Beweismittel eingeschleust hat.

Emmenés au poste de Paddington Green la veille après que la police a trouvé du cannabis dans l'appartement londonien de Ringo Starr sur Montagu Square, où ils logent, Lennon et Ono sont libérés sous caution par le tribunal de police de Marylebone, qui les inculpe de détention de cannabis et d'obstruction à l'exécution par la police d'un mandat de perquisition. Lennon plaide coupable de détention de cannabis et reçoit une amende de 150 livres sterling (assortie de 20 guinées de frais de dossier). Yoko est innocentée. Le sergent qui a procédé à leur arrestation, le détective Norman Pilcher, fera plus tard de la prison pour falsification de preuves dans plusieurs autres affaires.

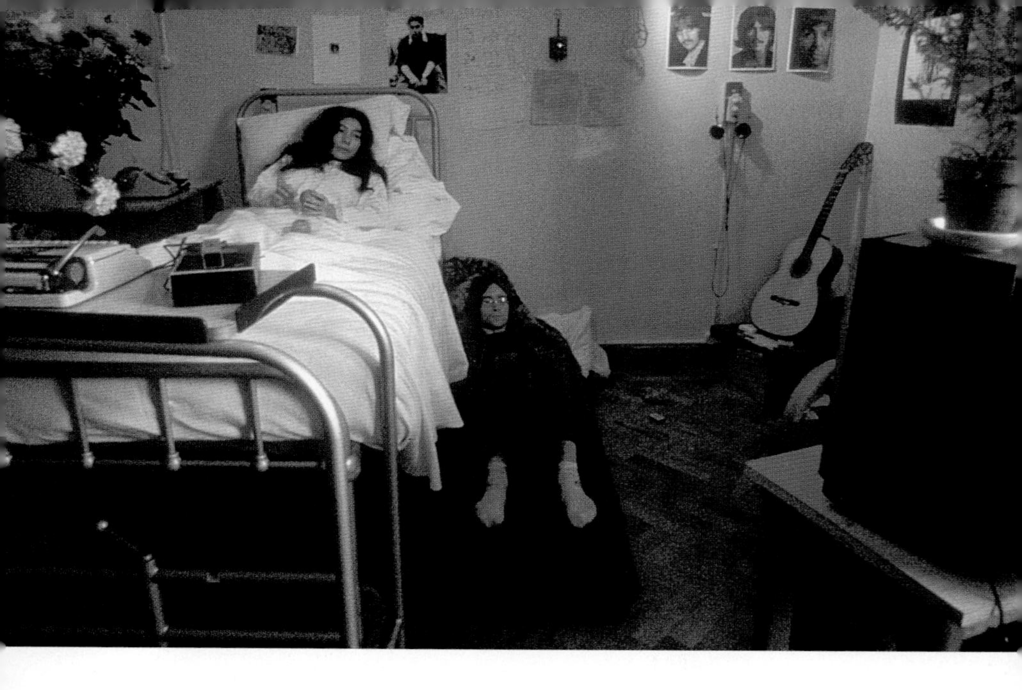

THURSDAY, NOVEMBER 21, 1968

Yoko suffers a miscarriage at Queen Charlotte's Children's Hospital in Hammersmith, London. John stays by her side, sleeping on the floor. On the wall are photographs of the other Beatles.

Yoko erleidet im Queen Charlotte's Children's Hospital in Hammersmith, London, eine Fehlgeburt. John bleibt die ganze Zeit bei ihr und schläft auf dem Boden. An der Wand hängen Fotos der anderen Beatles.

Yoko subit une fausse couche au Queen Charlotte's Children's Hospital de Hammersmith, à Londres. John reste à ses côtés et dort par terre. Il a accroché des photos des autres Beatles au mur.

FRIDAY, NOVEMBER 29, 1968

Although the increasingly fractured Beatles are still together (their double album ***The Beatles*** was issued last week), John and Yoko's first LP, ***Unfinished Music No. 1 – Two Virgins*** is released by the Beatles' own Apple label. Recorded the night he invited her to his Weybridge home, the album—a melange of sound effects and disjointed music—is made infamous by its cover which depicts the couple in a naked, full-frontal pose. Lennon took the photo himself on a delayed shutter release. Immediately controversial, the LP is shipped to retailers in plain brown paper bags.

Die Beatles sind zwar zerrüttet, aber noch zusammen (ihr Doppelalbum ***The Beatles*** kam in der Vorwoche auf den Markt), doch auf dem Beatles-eigenen Apple Label erscheint bereits die erste LP von John und Yoko: ***Unfinished Music No. 1 – Two Virgins***. Das Album wurde in der Nacht aufgenommen, in der er sie zu sich nach Weybridge einlud, und ist eine Mischung aus Klangeffekten und Musikfragmenten. Das Paar ist auf dem Cover in voller Frontalansicht nackt zu sehen, John Lennon hat das Foto mit Selbstauslöser aufgenommen. Die LP wird augenblicklich berühmt-berüchtigt. Die Auslieferung an die Händler erfolgt in unbedruckten braunen Papiertüten.

Alors que les Beatles, malgré des dissensions de plus en plus importantes, sont toujours ensemble (leur double album ***The Beatles*** est sorti la semaine précédente), John et Yoko sortent leur premier album conjoint, ***Unfinished Music Vol. 1 : Two Virgins*** sur le label Apple des Beatles. Enregistré la nuit où il a invité Yoko dans sa maison de Weybridge, le disque – un mélange d'effets sonores et de musique morcelée – fait scandale en raison de sa jaquette, qui montre le couple debout, de face, nu. Lennon a pris la photo lui-même grâce à un retardateur. L'album est envoyé aux détaillants dans une enveloppe de papier kraft.

"Foreign-made pornographic material. The pictures alone are not only obscene, but the wording on his particular piece of pornographic literature reads—'When two great Saints meet, it is a humbling experience.' This made the LP anti-Christian."

„Ausländisches pornografisches Material. Nicht nur die Bilder an sich sind obszön, sondern auch die Worte. In dieser pornografischen Literatur heißt es: ‚Wenn zwei große Heilige aufeinandertreffen, ist das eine Erfahrung, die einen demütig werden lässt.' Die LP ist aus diesem Grund antichristlich. "

« Il s'agit de matériel pornographique venu de l'étranger. Non seulement les photos elles-mêmes sont obscènes, mais cet exemple flagrant de littérature pornographique comporte notamment ces paroles : "Quand deux grands saints se rencontrent, c'est une leçon d'humilité." Cet album est donc antichrétien. »

LLOYD CRUSE, QUEBEC CONSERVATIVE MEMBER OF PARLIAMENT DESCRIBING TWO VIRGINS IN THE HOUSE OF COMMONS

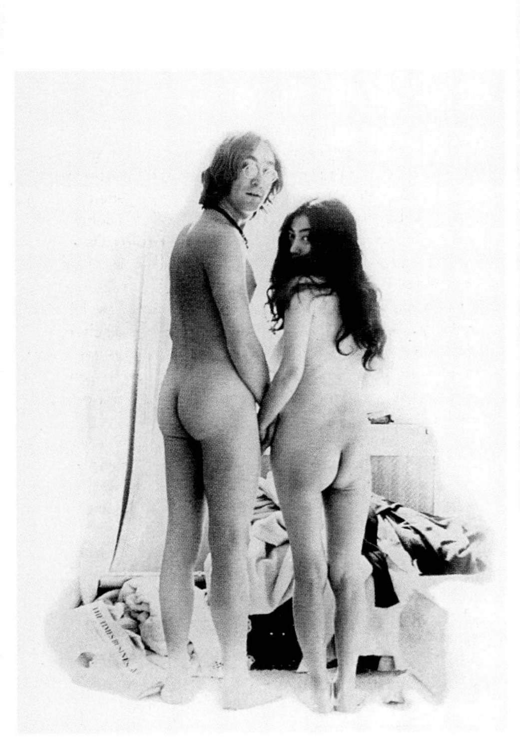

WEDNESDAY, DECEMBER 11, 1968

Lennon makes his first scheduled solo music television performance singing *Yer Blues* at the filming of "The Rolling Stones' Rock 'n' Roll Circus" project. Accompanied as ever by Yoko, the pair will continue in festive mood throughout the month, attending "A Hippy Gathering—An Alchemical Wedding" at the Royal Albert Hall in London, and then dressing up as Santa and Mrs. Claus at Apple's annual Christmas party.

John Lennon tritt zum ersten Mal solo im Fernsehen auf, wo er bei den Filmaufnahmen des Projekts „The Rolling Stones' Rock 'n' Roll Circus" *Yer Blues* singt. Yoko ist wie immer dabei, und das Paar verbringt den ganzen Monat in ausgelassener Stimmung, nimmt an „A Hippy Gathering – An Alchemical Wedding" in der Royal Albert Hall in London teil und verkleidet sich auf der Apple-Weihnachtsfeier als Santa und Mrs. Claus.

Lennon fait sa première apparition musicale en solo à la télévision sur le tournage du projet « The Rolling Stones' Rock 'n' Roll Circus ». Il chante *Yer Blues*, accompagné comme toujours par Yoko. Le couple enchaîne les événements mondains pendant tout le mois : il participe au « Hippy Gathering » (« Un mariage alchimique ») au Royal Albert Hall de Londres puis revêt les costumes du Père et de la Mère Noël à la fête de Noël d'Apple.

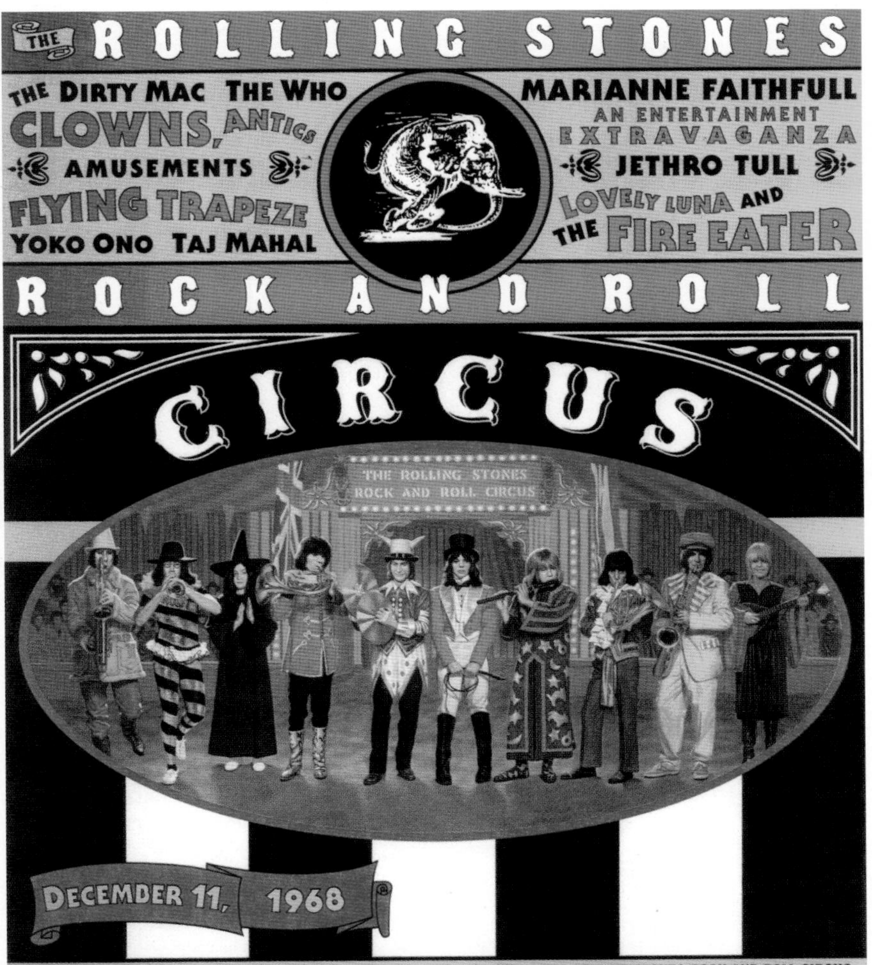
THE ROLLING STONES
THE DIRTY MAC THE WHO
CLOWNS, ANTICS
AMUSEMENTS
FLYING TRAPEZE
YOKO ONO TAJ MAHAL
MARIANNE FAITHFULL
AN ENTERTAINMENT
EXTRAVAGANZA
JETHRO TULL
LOVELY LUNA AND
THE FIRE EATER
ROCK AND ROLL
CIRCUS
THE ROLLING STONES
ROCK AND ROLL CIRCUS
DECEMBER 11, 1968
YOU'VE HEARD OF OXFORD CIRCUS; YOU'VE HEARD OF PICCADILLY CIRCUS; AND THIS IS THE ROLLING STONES ROCK AND ROLL CIRCUS;
AND WE'VE GOT SIGHTS AND SOUNDS AND MARVELS TO DELIGHT YOUR EYES AND EARS; AND YOU'LL BE ABLE TO HEAR THE VERY FIRST ONE OF THOSE IN A FEW MOMENTS.

FRIDAY, JANUARY 24, 1969

After 30,000 copies of ***Two Virgins*** were impounded three weeks ago as they were being unloaded from a plane at Newark Airport in Newark, New Jersey—the justification being the album's cover is "pornographic"—New Jersey's Union County Prosecutor Leo Kaplowitz issues a "don't sell or else" ultimatum to record dealers in connection with the record. Members of his staff and police seize 22,300 album covers—300 with records inside—from Bestway Products Company in Mountainside. Cleveland's city law director Clarence James will warn local distributors they would face prosecution if the record was not removed from record stores.

Drei Wochen zuvor wurden 30.000 Exemplare von5***Two Virgins*** beim Entladen eines Flugzeugs am Flughafen von Newark, New Jersey, beschlagnahmt – mit der Begründung, das Cover sei „pornografisch". Der Staatsanwalt des Union County in New Jersey, Leo Kaplowitz, ordnet unter Strafandrohung ein Verkaufsverbot des Albums an. Seine Mitarbeiter und Polizisten beschlagnahmen 22.300 Plattenhüllen bei der Bestway Products Company in Mountainside – 300 davon mit Schallplatten darin. Clevelands Gerichtspräsident Clarence James warnt die örtlichen Plattenhändler, dass sie juristisch belangt würden, wenn die Platte nicht aus den Läden der Stadt verschwinde.

Trois semaines plus tôt, 30 000 exemplaires de ***Two Virgins*** ont été saisis alors qu'ils étaient déchargés d'un avion à l'aéroport de Newark (New Jersey) – la couverture de l'album étant jugée « pornographique ». Le procureur du comté du New Jersey Leo Kaplowitz menace les disquaires de représailles s'ils mettent l'album en vente. Les membres de son équipe et la police saisissent 22 300 pochettes – et seulement 300 disques – dans les locaux de la Bestway Products Company, à Mountainside. Le responsable des autorités judiciaires de Cleveland Clarence James avertit les distributeurs locaux qu'ils seront poursuivis s'ils ne retirent pas le disque des bacs.

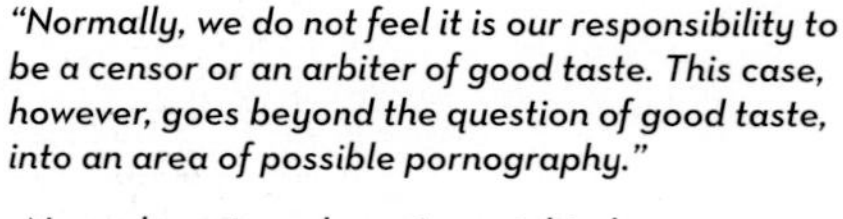

"Normally, we do not feel it is our responsibility to be a censor or an arbiter of good taste. This case, however, goes beyond the question of good taste, into an area of possible pornography."

„Normalerweise sehen wir es nicht als unsere Verantwortung an, uns als Zensor oder Schiedsrichter in Geschmacksfragen zu betätigen. In diesem Fall wurden die Grenzen des guten Geschmacks jedoch eindeutig überschritten und es handelt sich eventuell sogar um Pornografie."

« Nous n'avons pas pour habitude de nous considérer comme des censeurs ou des arbitres du bon goût. Cependant ce cas dépasse largement la question du bon goût pour entrer dans le domaine de la pornographie potentielle. »

DAVID LIEBERMAN, PRESIDENT OF LIEBERMAN ENTERPRISES, A MAJOR RECORD WHOLESALER

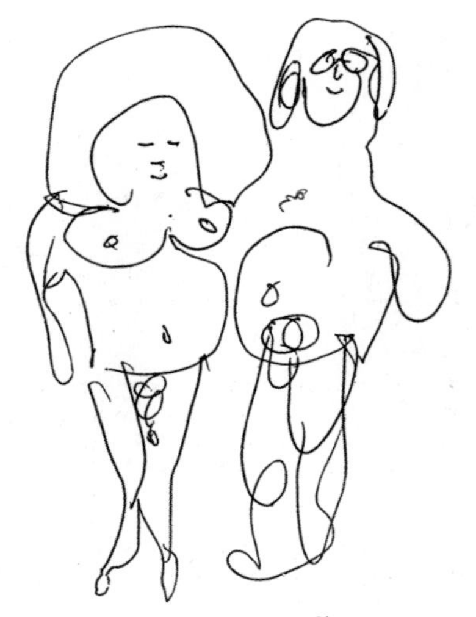

"I'd like to say 'thank you' on behalf of the group and ourselves, and I hope we passed the audition."

„Ich möchte mich im Namen der Gruppe und uns selbst bedanken – und ich hoffe, wir haben das Vorspielen bestanden."

« J'aimerais vous remercier au nom du groupe et de nous-mêmes, et j'espère que nous avons réussi l'audition ».

JOHN LENNON

THURSDAY, JANUARY 30, 1969

Conceived at a meeting on Sunday, the Beatles perform on the roof of the Apple building at 3, Savile Row, London. The historic jam is halted by police after 42 minutes following a noise complaint by Stephen King, chief accountant of the nearby Royal Bank of Scotland. Finishing with *Get Back*, it will prove to be the last time the Beatles perform together in public. With Lennon now inseparable from Ono—and with deep personality and artistic conflicts widening the divide amongst band members—the Beatles will dissolve by year's end, making their final recording as a quartet on *I Want You (She's So Heavy)* on August 20.

Bei einem Treffen am Sonntag planen die Beatles das Konzert, das an diesem Tag auf dem Dach des Apple-Gebäudes in der Savile Row 3 in London stattfindet. Dieser Spontanauftritt wird nach 42 Minuten von der Polizei unterbrochen. Die Band beschließt ihren Auftritt mit *Get Back*; es soll das letzte Mal bleiben, dass die Beatles öffentlich zusammen auftreten. John Lennon und Yoko Ono sind mittlerweile unzertrennlich, und tiefe persönliche und künstlerische Konflikte vergrößern den Graben zwischen den Band-Mitgliedern. Die Beatles lösen sich Ende des Jahres endgültig auf und machen ihre letzte Plattenaufnahme als Quartett am 20. August: *I Want You (She's So Heavy)*.

Les Beatles donnent un concert historique sur le toit du siège d'Apple, à Londres. Il est interrompu par la police au bout de 42 minutes. Le set se termine sur *Get Back* ; c'est la dernière fois que les Beatles se produisent ensemble en public. Lennon est devenu inséparable d'Ono et les conflits artistiques entre les membres du groupe s'aggravent. Le groupe finira par se séparer cette année-là, après un dernier enregistrement collectif, celui de *I Want You (She's So Heavy)*, le 20 août.

SUNDAY, MARCH 2, 1969

500 attendees at an evening of experimental music at the Lady Mitchell Hall, Cambridge University are surprised when an unannounced John and Yoko step onto the stage and perform an improvised piece, which will be subsequently titled *Cambridge 1969*, and feature on their ***Unfinished Music No. 2 – Life With The Lions***, set for release on May 9. Another attempt at avant-garde experimentalism, it will include a recording made on a cassette player during Yoko's recent hospital stay.

500 Besucher eines Abends für experimentelle Musik in der Lady Mitchell Hall an der Cambridge University sind erstaunt, als John und Yoko unangekündigt die Bühne betreten und ein improvisiertes Stück aufführen, das später den Titel *Cambridge 1969* erhält und auf ihrem Album ***Unfinished Music No. 2 – Life With The Lions*** am 9. Mai herauskommt. Es ist ein Avantgarde-Experiment, bei dem auch eine Aufnahme auf einem Kassettenrekorder vorkommt, die während Yokos Krankenhausaufenthalt entstanden ist.

Les 500 spectateurs venus assister à un concert de musique expérimentale au Lady Mitchell Hall de l'université de Cambridge ont la surprise de voir John et Yoko monter sur scène, sans être annoncés, et improviser un morceau plus tard intitulé *Cambridge 1969* et intégré à ***Unfinished Music Vol. 2 : Life With The Lions***, qui doit sortir le 9 mai. Nouvelle tentative expérimentale d'avant-garde, l'album contient notamment un enregistrement réalisé sur un magnétophone à cassette pendant le récent séjour de Yoko à l'hôpital.

THURSDAY, MARCH 20, 1969

John marries Yoko in the British Consulate office in Gibraltar. Registrar Cecil Wheeler officiates. After the brief ceremony, the couple pose for photographs in the shadow of the Rock of Gibraltar, before heading back to Paris, to begin their honeymoon.

John Lennon heiratet Yoko Ono auf dem britischen Konsulat in Gibraltar, Standesbeamter ist Cecil Wheeler. Nach der kurzen Amtshandlung lässt sich das Paar im Schatten des Felsens von Gibraltar fotografieren und fliegt dann zurück nach Paris in die Flitterwochen.

John Lennon épouse Yoko Ono au consulat britannique à Gibraltar, en présence du fonctionnaire de l'état civil Cecil Wheeler. Après une brève cérémonie, le couple pose pour les photographes à l'ombre du rocher de Gibraltar, avant de gagner Paris pour y entamer leur lune de miel.

TUESDAY, MARCH 25, 1969

Having driven from Paris to Amsterdam, the newlyweds begin a week-long "bed-in" promoting world peace, in Room 902 on the ninth floor of the presidential suite of the Hilton Hotel. Under the hand-written slogans "Hair Peace" and "Bed Peace," the pair hold a press conference in their pyjamas.

Das frisch verheiratete Paar fährt von Paris nach Amsterdam, wo es sein einwöchiges „Bed-In" für den Weltfrieden in Zimmer 902 der Präsidentensuite im 9. Stock des Hilton Hotel beginnt. Sie halten unter den handgeschriebenen Slogans „Hair Peace" und „Bed Peace" eine Pressekonferenz in Schlafanzügen ab.

Les jeunes mariés vont en voiture de Paris à Amsterdam et entament leur fameux « bed-in » pour la paix mondiale dans la suite présidentielle de l'hôtel Hilton, chambre 902, au neuvième étage. Le couple accueille la presse en pyjama sous les slogans « Hair Peace » et « Bed Peace » écrits à la main.

HAI
PEAC

BED
PEACE.

TUESDAY, APRIL 1, 1969
Having flown from Amsterdam to Vienna yesterday for a press conference coinciding with the world premiere of their new film "The Rape," they now appear on the Eamonn Andrews-hosted "Today" program on ITV. They will be seen again on Andrews' late-night show on Thursday.

Die beiden sind am Vortag von Amsterdam nach Wien zu einer Pressekonferenz geflogen. Anlass ist die Weltpremiere ihres neuen Films „The Rape". An diesem Tag sind sie in der Fernsehsendung „Today" bei Moderator Eamonn Andrews zu Gast. Am Donnerstag sind sie noch einmal in Andrews' Spätabendsendung zu sehen.

Arrivé à Vienne la veille pour une conférence de presse organisée pour la sortie mondiale de leur nouveau film, « The Rape », le couple participe à l'émission d'ITV « Today », présentée par Eamonn Andrews. Ils viendront aussi dans l'émission de fin de soirée de l'animateur, le jeudi.

TUESDAY, APRIL 22, 1969
On the roof of the Apple building in Savile Row, London, Lennon adds Ono to his middle name by deed poll, in a ceremony conducted by Commissioner of Oaths Señor Bueno de Mesquita.

In einer von Notar Señor Bueno de Mesquita geleiteten Zeremonie auf dem Dach des Apple-Gebäudes in der Savile Row in London nimmt John Lennon „Ono" als dritten Vornamen an.

Sur le toit d'Apple sur Savile Row, à Londres, Lennon remplace son deuxième prénom par Ono dans un acte unilatéral, au cours d'une cérémonie menée par le « commissaire aux serments » Bueno de Mesquita.

"I was always cut off from average people, even before I was a Beatle. I've never been normal, or so-called normal. I was never a lorry driver or a clerk and I had no intention of being one as soon as I found out what they were as a kid."

„Ich war immer schon von der Durchschnittsbevölkerung abgeschnitten, auch als ich noch kein Beatle war. Ich bin noch nie normal gewesen oder das, was man normal nennt. Ich war nie Fernfahrer oder Büroangestellter und mir war schon als Kind klar, dass ich nie so werden wollte."

« J'ai toujours été coupé des gens ordinaires, même avant de faire partie des Beatles. Je n'ai jamais été normal, ou ce qu'on appelle normal. Je n'ai jamais été chauffeur routier ou employé et je n'ai jamais eu l'intention de le devenir, pas après avoir compris en quoi ces métiers consistaient, quand j'étais gamin. »

JOHN LENNON, MELODY MAKER, APRIL 12, 1969

MONDAY, MAY 26, 1969

The Lennons begin another "bed-in" to promote world peace in Room 1742 of the Hotel La Reine Elizabeth in Montreal, Canada, once again opening the event to the media. Originally planning to bed down in New York, the location was changed after United States authorities canceled Lennon's non-immigrant visa.

Die Lennons führen ein zweites „Bed-In" für den Weltfrieden in Zimmer 1742 des Hotels La Reine Elizabeth in Montreal, Kanada, durch, das wieder ein großes Medienereignis wird. Eigentlich hatten sie sich in New York ins Bett legen wollen, doch die amerikanische Einwanderungsbehörde hatte Lennons Besuchervisum für ungültig erklärt.

Les Lennon inaugurent leur deuxième « bed-in » pacifiste dans la chambre 1742 de l'hôtel La Reine Elizabeth à Montréal (Canada), une fois encore sous le regard de la presse. Le couple comptait organiser l'événement à New York mais a dû changer de lieu après l'annulation du visa de Lennon par les autorités américaines.

SUNDAY, JUNE 1, 1969

At the end of their week-long "bed-in," the Lennons are joined by the Smothers Brothers, Petula Clark, Derek Taylor, Timothy Leary, the Canadian Radha Krishna Temple, self-anointed fifth Beatle Murray the K, Rabbi Abraham Feinberg and some 50 fans outside the hotel to take part in a recording of the just-written *Give Peace A Chance*. The impromptu session has been organized by Capitol Records (Canada) A&R executive, Pierre Dubord who enlists engineer Andre Perry to record it on portable 8-track equipment. The song will become a clarion call for the anti-war movement and in November an estimated 250,000 people will sing it in Washington, DC, at a rally protesting the Vietnam War.

Zum Abschluss ihres einwöchigen „Bed-Ins" gesellen sich die Smothers Brothers, Petula Clark, Derek Taylor, Timothy Leary, Mitglieder des kanadischen Radha Krishna Tempels, der selbst ernannte fünfte Beatle Murray the K, Rabbi Abraham Feinberg und an die 50 Fans vor dem Hotel zu den Lennons und nehmen an der Einspielung des gerade geschriebenen Songs *Give Peace A Chance* teil. Die Spontansession wurde vom A&R-Chef bei Capitol Records (Canada) Pierre Dubord organisiert; er hat den Toningenieur Andre Perry angeheuert, der das Ganze mit einer tragbaren Tonbandausrüstung aufnimmt. Das Lied entwickelt sich zur inoffiziellen Hymne der Vietnamkriegsgegner: Im November singen es geschätzte 250.000 Teilnehmer einer Demonstration gegen den Vietnamkrieg in Washington, D.C.

À l'issue de leur semaine militante au lit, les Lennon sont rejoints dans leur chambre par les Smothers Brothers, Petula Clark, Derek Taylor, Timothy Leary, le Temple canadien de Radha Krishna, l'autoproclamé cinquième Beatle Murray the K et le rabbin Abraham Feinberg, ainsi qu'une cinquantaine de fans réunis devant l'hôtel, pour enregistrer *Give Peace A Chance*, que Lennon vient de composer. Ce bœuf « impromptu » a en fait été organisé par le responsable du département Artistes et Répertoire de Capitol Records (Canada), Pierre Dubord, qui demande à l'ingénieur du son Andre Perry de l'enregistrer sur un équipement 8 pistes portable. La chanson devient l'hymne du mouvement pacifiste et en novembre, environ 250 000 personnes l'entonnent à Washington lors d'un rassemblement contre la guerre du Vietnam.

TUESDAY, JULY 1, 1969

The Lennons are taken to Lawson Memorial Hospital after a car accident in Golspie, Scotland, whilst on vacation. John receives 17 stitches for a facial wound, Yoko 14 and her daughter, Kyoko four, while Julian Lennon is treated for shock.

Die Lennons werden nach einem Autounfall im Urlaub in Golspie, Schottland, ins Lawson Memorial Hospital gebracht. John muss mit 17 Stichen im Gesicht genäht werden, Yoko mit 14, ihre Tochter Kyoko mit vier, Julian Lennon hat einen Schock erlitten.

Les Lennon sont hospitalisés au Lawson Memorial après avoir eu un accident de voiture à Golspie, en Écosse, où ils passent leurs vacances. John reçoit 17 points de suture pour une blessure au visage, Yoko 14 et sa fille Kyoko, quatre ; Julian Lennon est en état de choc, mais indemne.

WEDNESDAY, SEPTEMBER 10, 1969

"An Evening With John And Yoko" takes place at the New Cinema Club at the ICA in London. They show four short films while sitting in a bag beside the screen, also taking questions from the assembled audience.

Im New Cinema Club im ICA in London findet „An Evening With John And Yoko" statt. Sie zeigen vier Kurzfilme, während sie in einem Sack neben der Leinwand sitzen und Fragen aus dem Publikum beantworten.

Soirée « An Evening With John And Yoko » au New Cinema Club de l'ICA, à Londres : le couple présente quatre courts métrages, assis dans un sac à côté de l'écran et répond aux questions du public.

"Stressing their intentions to spread peace, the husband and wife team contributed six tunes ... Lennon energetically jumped and danced while Miss Ono alternated between climbing into a large white sack and kissing her husband."

„Das aus dem Ehepaar Lennon bestehende Team steuerte sechs Stücke bei, wobei es seine Absicht kundtat, zur Verbreitung des Friedens beizutragen ... Lennon sprang und tanzte energiegeladen herum, während Miss Ono abwechselnd in einen großen weißen Sack kletterte und ihren Mann küsste."

« Toujours engagés dans la diffusion de leur message de paix, mari et femme ont joué six titres. [...] Lennon, plein d'énergie, bondissait sur scène tandis que Mlle Ono grimpait dans un grand sac blanc ou embrassait son mari. »

VARIETY, SEPTEMBER 17, 1969

"We're going to do numbers we know, 'cause we never played together before."

„Wir spielen ein paar Stücke, die wir kennen, weil wir noch nie zusammen gespielt haben."

« On va jouer des morceaux qu'on connaît, parce qu'on n'a jamais joué ensemble avant. »

JOHN LENNON

SATURDAY, SEPTEMBER 13, 1969

Invited by promoter John Brower to attend the "Toronto Rock 'n' Revival Show" held at Toronto University's Varsity Stadium in Canada, with the offer of first class airline tickets, Lennon agrees, providing he can perform. Assembling the ad-hoc Plastic Ono Band, he corrals Eric Clapton, Klaus Voormann and Alan White to join him. Having rehearsed during the flight, they play six numbers, including *Give Peace A Chance* and well-worn classics such as *Blue Suede Shoes* and *Dizzy Miss Lizzy*. Also on the bill are such rock legends as Chuck Berry, Jerry Lee Lewis, Little Richard and Gene Vincent.

John Lennon wird von Promoter John Brower eingeladen, bei der „Toronto Rock 'n' Revival Show" zu spielen, die im Varsity Stadium der Toronto University in Kanada stattfinden soll. Auf das Angebot von Erste-Klasse-Flugtickets hin sagt John zu und stellt spontan die Plastic Ono Band aus Eric Clapton, Klaus Voormann und Alan White zusammen. Sie proben erstmals während des Fluges und spielen sechs Stücke, darunter *Give Peace A Chance* und Evergreens wie *Blue Suede Shoes* und *Dizzy Miss Lizzy*. Bei dem Konzert treten Rocklegenden wie Chuck Berry, Jerry Lee Lewis, Little Richard und Gene Vincent auf.

Invité à assister au « Rock 'n' Revival Show » au Varsity Stadium de l'université de Toronto (Canada) par le promoteur de concerts John Brower, qui propose même de lui envoyer des billets d'avion en première classe, Lennon accepte à condition de pouvoir monter sur scène. Il réunit le Plastic Ono Band et convainc Eric Clapton, Klaus Voormann et Alan White de se joindre à eux. Le groupe répète dans l'avion et joue six titres, dont *Give Peace A Chance* et quelques classiques comme *Blue Suede Shoes* et *Dizzy Miss Lizzy*. Ils partagent l'affiche avec des légendes du rock comme Chuck Berry, Jerry Lee Lewis, Little Richard et Gene Vincent.

"It gave me a great feeling; a feeling I haven't had for a long time. It convinced me to do more appearances, either with or without the rest of the Beatles. Everything went down so well."

„Es war ein wunderbares Gefühl: So gut habe ich mich schon lange nicht mehr gefühlt. Es hat mich davon überzeugt, weitere Auftritte zu machen, mit oder ohne die anderen Beatles. Es ist alles super gelaufen."

« J'ai vécu un moment très fort, une sensation que je n'avais pas ressentie depuis très longtemps. Tout ça m'a convaincu de faire davantage de concerts, avec ou sans les autres Beatles. Tout s'est bien passé. »

JOHN LENNON TO ROLLING STONE WRITER RITCHIE YORKE AT APPLE'S LONDON OFFICES, TUESDAY SEPTEMBER 16, 1969

THURSDAY, SEPTEMBER 25, 1969
John and Yoko, Eric Clapton, Klaus Voormann and Ringo Starr begin recording the Plastic Ono Band's *Cold Turkey* in Studio Three at EMI's Abbey Road studios. They will return on Sunday to cut another version.

John und Yoko, Eric Clapton, Klaus Voormann und Ringo Starr beginnen mit den Aufnahmen zu *Cold Turkey* der Plastic Ono Band im Studio 3 der EMI Abbey Road Studios. Am Sonntag kehren sie noch einmal zurück, um eine zweite Version einzuspielen.

John et Yoko, Eric Clapton, Klaus Voormann et Ringo Starr commencent l'enregistrement de la chanson du Plastic Ono Band *Cold Turkey* au Studio Three d'EMI, à Abbey Road. Ils reviendront faire une deuxième version le dimanche.

TUESDAY, NOVEMBER 25, 1969
Increasingly vocal and radical in his political views, Lennon returns his MBE to Buckingham Palace with a note: "Your Majesty, I am returning this MBE in protest against Britain's involvement in the Nigeria-Biafra thing, against our support of America in Vietnam, and against *Cold Turkey* slipping down the charts. With love, John Lennon of Bag."

John Lennon äußert seine politischen Ansichten immer radikaler und schickt seinen MBE-Orden begleitet von einem Brief an den Buckingham Palace zurück: „Eure Majestät, ich gebe diesen MBE aus Protest gegen die Verwicklung Großbritanniens in die Sache mit Nigeria-Biafra, gegen unsere Unterstützung Amerikas im Vietnamkrieg und gegen das Abrutschen von *Cold Turkey* in den Charts zurück. Alles Liebe, John Lennon of Bag."

Lennon, dont les convictions politiques sont plus affirmées et radicales que jamais, renvoie sa nomination au titre de membre de l'Ordre très excellent de l'Empire britannique à Buckingham Palace avec le message suivant : « Votre Majesté, je vous retourne ce MBE pour protester contre l'ingérance de la Grande-Bretagne dans cette affaire entre le Nigéria et le Biafra, contre le soutien que vous apportez à l'Amérique au Vietnam, et contre la baisse des ventes de *Cold Turkey*. Avec toute mon affection, John Lennon de Bag. »

FRIDAY, NOVEMBER 14, 1969

The Wedding Album, another avant-garde offering which includes souvenirs of Lennon's wedding, is released. **Melody Maker**'s Richard Williams reviewing a pre-release copy of the album, pressed on two discs, each with a blank B-side, notes that these B-sides contain single tones "maintained throughout, presumably produced electronically. The pitch of the tones alters frequently, but only by microtones or, at most a semitone. This oscillation produces an almost subliminal uneven 'beat' which maintains interest." (They are, in fact, merely an engineer's test signal.)

The Wedding Album kommt auf den Markt, eine weitere Avantgarde-Produktion mit Souvenirs von der Hochzeit der beiden. Richard Williams vom **Melody Maker** schreibt in einer Kritik über ein Vorabexemplar, das auf zwei Schallplatten gepresst wurde, die beide leere B-Seiten haben: „Die B-Seiten enthalten einzelne Töne, die die ganze Zeit durchgehalten werden und vermutlich elektronisch produziert wurden. Die Tonhöhe ändert sich häufig, aber nur minimal, höchstens ein Halbton. Durch diese Oszillation entsteht ein unterschwelliger unregelmäßiger ‚Beat', der das Interesse wachhält." (In Wirklichkeit handelt es sich nur um das Testsignal des Toningenieurs.)

Sortie de ***The Wedding Album***, nouvel opus d'avant-garde comportant notamment des souvenirs du mariage de Lennon. Le critique de **Melody Maker** Richard Williams a écouté une version provisoire de l'album enregistrée sur deux disques dont les faces B, vierges de toute chanson, ne proposent que des sortes de notes « tenues, sans doute produites par l'électronique. La tonalité de ces signaux varie fréquemment, mais seulement par micro-intervalles ou, au plus, par demi-tons. Cette oscillation produit une pulsation irrégulière presque subliminale qui maintient l'intérêt ». (Il s'agit en fait de réglages effectués par un ingénieur du son.)

TUESDAY, DECEMBER 2, 1969

John and Yoko are filmed at their Tittenhurst Park home as subjects for the ITV documentary, "Man Of The Decade," airing on December 30. Lennon has been nominated by noted zoologist and ethologist, Desmond Morris. Meanwhile, BBC1-TV begins a five-day shoot for "The World Of John And Yoko" which will broadcast on December 15, hosted by David Dimbleby.

John und Yoko werden in ihrer Villa in Tittenhurst Park für den ITV-Dokumentarfilm „Man Of The Decade" gefilmt, der am 30. Dezember ausgestrahlt wird. John Lennon wurde von dem anerkannten Zoologen und Verhaltensforscher Desmond Morris vorgeschlagen. Gleichzeitig beginnt BBC1 mit fünftägigen Dreharbeiten für „The World Of John And Yoko", ein Feature mit Moderator David Dimbleby, das am 15. Dezember ausgestrahlt wird.

John et Yoko sont filmés dans leur maison de Tittenhurst Park pour un documentaire diffusé sur ITV le 30 décembre intitulé « Homme de la décennie ». Lennon a été choisi par le célèbre zoologiste et éthologiste Desmond Morris. Dans le même temps, la chaîne BBC1 entame cinq jours de tournage pour « The World Of John And Yoko », qui passe à l'antenne le 15 décembre, présenté par David Dimbleby.

THURSDAY, DECEMBER 11, 1969

Lennon attends the Royal Charity premiere of "The Magic Christian" at the Odeon Theatre in Kensington, carrying the placard "Britain Murdered Hanratty." James Hanratty was a small-time crook hanged in 1962 for the murder of Michael Gregsten. Many thought his conviction was unsafe and that he was innocent of the crime, which led to a cause celebre throughout the decade. (In 2001, his body will be exhumed so that a DNA sample can be taken for analysis. The conclusion: Hanratty was guilty.)

John Lennon besucht die Royal Charity-Premiere von „The Magic Christian" im Odeon Theatre in Kensington, in der Hand das Plakat „Britain Murdered Hanratty". James Hanratty war ein Kleinkrimineller, der 1962 wegen des Mordes an Michael Gregsten gehängt wurde. Er wurde von vielen als unschuldig und seine Verurteilung als nicht rechtmäßig angesehen, was das ganze Jahrzehnt über für viel Medienaufmerksamkeit sorgte. (2001 wird sein Leichnam exhumiert und eine DNA-Probe entnommen und analysiert, Ergebnis: Hanratty war schuldig.)

Lennon assiste à la première de « The Magic Christian », une soirée au profit de la Royal Charity Association, à l'Odeon Theatre de Kensington ; il arbore une pancarte « la Grande-Bretagne a tué Hanratty ». James Hanratty était un escroc à la petite semaine qui fut pendu en 1962 pour le meurtre de Michael Gregsten. Pour beaucoup, sa condamnation ne reposait pas sur des preuves solides et le jeune homme était innocent. (L'enquête a été rouverte en 2001, le corps d'Hanratty a été exhumé et les analyses ADN ont confirmé sa culpabilité.)

MONDAY, DECEMBER 15, 1969

The Plastic Ono Band makes its United Kingdom performance debut, headlining the UNICEF "Peace For Christmas" benefit concert at London's Lyceum Ballroom. Put together at 48 hours' notice, Ono Band veterans Lennon, Ono, Clapton, Voormann and White are augmented by George Harrison, Bobby Keyes, Billy Preston, Keith Moon, Jim Gordon and Delaney & Bonnie. The concert sees two Beatles on stage together for the first time since May 1, 1966—with Lennon making what will prove to be his last ever live appearance in Britain.

Die Plastic Ono Band tritt zum ersten Mal in England auf. Sie spielt als Headliner beim UNICEF-Benefizkonzert „Peace For Christmas" im Londoner Lyceum Ballroom. Die Band wird innerhalb von 48 Stunden zusammengestellt, aus den alten Ono-Bandmitgliedern Lennon, Ono, Clapton, Voormann und White und außerdem George Harrison, Bobby Keyes, Billy Preston, Keith Moon, Jim Gordon und Delaney & Bonnie. Bei dem Konzert stehen zum ersten Mal seit dem 1. Mai 1966 wieder zwei Beatles zusammen auf der Bühne – für John Lennon ist es der letzte Live-Auftritt in Großbritannien.

Le Plastic Ono Band fait ses premiers pas sur la scène musicale britannique en ouverture du concert de bienfaisance de l'UNICEF « Peace For Christmas », au Lyceum Ballroom de Londres. Prévenus de l'événement seulement 48 heures plus tôt, les vétérans du groupe (Lennon, Ono, Clapton, Voormann et White) sont accompagnés de George Harrison, Bobby Keyes, Billy Preston, Keith Moon, Jim Gordon et Delaney & Bonnie. Deux Beatles partagent la scène pour la première fois depuis le 1er mai 1966. (Ce concert sera aussi le dernier de Lennon sur le territoire britannique.)

"So I refuse to be leader, and I'll always show my genitals or do something which prevents me from being Martin Luther King or Gandhi and getting killed."

„Ich weigere mich, als Führerfigur aufzutreten, und ich werde immer meine Genitalien zeigen oder irgendetwas machen, was mich davor bewahrt, Martin Luther King oder Gandhi zu sein und ermordet zu werden."

« Je refuse d'être un leader et je persisterai à montrer mes parties génitales ou à faire autre chose qui m'empêchera d'être un nouveau Martin Luther King ou Gandhi… et de me faire tuer. »

JOHN LENNON, MELODY MAKER, DECEMBER 13, 1969

TUESDAY, DECEMBER 16, 1969

"War Is Over! – If You Want It – Happy Christmas from John & Yoko" billboards go up in London, New York, Paris, Rome, Berlin, Athens, Amsterdam, Los Angeles, Montreal and Toronto.

Plakatwände mit der Aufschrift: „War Is Over! – If You Want It – Happy Christmas John And Yoko" erscheinen in London, New York, Paris, Rom, Berlin, Athen, Amsterdam, Los Angeles, Montreal und Toronto.

Le message « War Is Over! – If You Want It – Happy Christmas John And Yoko » (« La guerre est finie ! Si vous le voulez. Joyeux Noël. John et Yoko ») est placardé sur les murs de Londres, New York, Paris, Rome, Berlin, Athènes, Amsterdam, Los Angeles, Montréal et Toronto.

WAR IS
IF YOU
Happy
US

OVER!
T IT
ADWAY
U.S ARM
ARINE CORPS

LA
GUERRE
EST FINIE!
LA
GUERRE
EST FINIE!
WAR
IS
OVER!

"If I have to pay for the other Beatles to come to it, I will."

„Wenn ich dafür bezahlen muss, dass die anderen Beatles mit dabei sind, werde ich das tun."

« Si je dois payer pour que les autres Beatles nous rejoignent, je le ferai. »

JOHN LENNON

WEDNESDAY, DECEMBER 17, 1969

A day after arriving in Toronto, the Lennons hold a press conference to announce their involvement in a peace concert in Mosport Park next July 3 through 5. They stay at Ronnie Hawkins' farm nearby during their visit, which will see them leave Canada on Christmas Day. (When they subsequently discover in March that festival organizer John Brower will be charging admission to the concert, the Lennons will pull out.)

Einen Tag nach der Ankunft in Toronto halten die Lennons eine Pressekonferenz ab, bei der sie ihre Teilnahme an einem Friedenskonzert im Mosport Park vom 3. bis 5. Juli 1970 bekannt geben. Sie wohnen auf der Farm von Ronnie Hawkins und verlassen Kanada am ersten Weihnachtsfeiertag. (Als sie im März herausfinden, dass der Festivalausrichter John Brower Eintritt für das Konzert verlangen will, sagen sie ihre Teilnahme ab.)

Le lendemain de leur arrivée à Toronto, les Lennon tiennent une conférence de presse pour annoncer leur participation à un concert pacifiste au Mosport Park du 3 au 5 juillet de l'année suivante. Ils logent dans la ferme de Ronnie Hawkins et quittent le Canada le jour de Noël. (En mars, lorsqu'ils découvriront que l'organisateur du festival, John Brower, compte faire payer l'entrée, les Lennon se retireront du projet.)

TUESDAY, DECEMBER 23, 1969

John and Yoko attend a 50-minute closed door meeting with Canadian Prime Minister, Pierre Trudeau, after which Lennon says, "If all politicians were like Mr. Trudeau, then there would be world peace."

John und Yoko haben eine private, fünfzigminütige Unterredung mit dem kanadischen Premierminister Pierre Trudeau. John sagt hinterher: „Wenn alle Politiker so wären wie Mr. Trudeau, dann hätten wir Weltfrieden."

John et Yoko rencontrent le Premier ministre canadien Pierre Trudeau pour un entretien privé de 50 minutes, à l'issue duquel Lennon déclare : « Si tous les politiciens étaient comme M. Trudeau, le monde serait en paix ».

THE 1970s

DIE 1970ER

LES ANNÉES 1970

MONDAY, JANUARY 5, 1970

Staying with Yoko's ex-husband Tony Cox in Denmark, the Lennons hold a press conference at which they reveal that all future proceeds from their disks and songs will go toward promoting peace on earth. They also send two saplings to Israeli Prime Minister, Golda Meir to plant in her garden. After finding out who John and Yoko are, she will agree to plant them. During their stay, local hairdresser Aase Haugkrogh will shorn them of their flowing locks.

Die Lennons wohnen bei Yokos Exmann Tony Cox in Dänemark, wo sie bei einer Pressekonferenz bekannt geben, dass alle zukünftigen Einnahmen aus ihren Schallplatten und Liedern für die Verbreitung des Friedens auf Erden verwendet werden sollen. Sie schicken zwei Baumsetzlinge an die israelische Premierministerin Golda Meir für ihren Garten. Nachdem diese in Erfahrung gebracht hat, wer John und Yoko sind, erklärt sie sich zum Einpflanzen bereit. In Dänemark lassen sich beide von Friseurin Aase Haugkrogh die Haarpracht abschneiden.

Hébergés par Tony Cox, l'ex-mari de Yoko, au Danemark, les Lennon tiennent une conférence de presse au cours de laquelle ils annoncent que tous les bénéfices qui découleront désormais de leurs disques et de leurs chansons seront consacrés à la défense et à la promotion de la paix dans le monde. Ils envoient par ailleurs deux arbustes au Premier ministre israélien Golda Meir qui, après s'être fait expliquer qui sont John et Yoko, accepte de les planter dans son jardin. Au cours de leur séjour, le coiffeur local Aase Haugkrogh les déleste tous deux de leurs cheveux longs.

FRIDAY, JANUARY 16, 1970

"Bag One," an exhibition of John Lennon's erotic lithographs at the London Art Gallery in New Bond Street, is raided by police acting under the Obscene Publications Act. They seize eight of Lennon's lithographs—deeming them pornographic. Three weeks into the trial, the magistrate will dismiss the case on the grounds that the Metropolitan Police Act of 1839, which makes it an offence to distribute indecent material in a thoroughfare, was not violated as the art gallery does not constitute a thoroughfare.

„Bag One", eine Ausstellung mit John Lennons erotischen Lithographien in der London Art Gallery, New Bond Street, wird von der Polizei im Rahmen des „Gesetzes über obszöne Veröffentlichungen" gestürmt, acht der Lennon-Drucke werden als pornografisch beschlagnahmt. Nach dreiwöchiger Verhandlung weist der Richter die Klage ab, Begründung: Der Metropolitan Police Act von 1839 verbietet die Verbreitung obszöner Materialien nur an Durchgangsstraßen, und die Galerie stellt keine Durchgangsstraße dar.

« Bag One, » une exposition de lithographies érotiques signées John Lennon organisée à la London Art Gallery, sur New Bond Street, est interrompue par la police en vertu de l'Obscene Publications Act. Elle saisit huit lithographies jugées pornographiques. Au bout de trois semaines de procès, les avocats de Lennon font classer l'affaire en s'appuyant sur le Metropolitan Police Act de 1839, qui précise qu'il n'y a délit que si les documents obscènes sont montrés dans un lieu de passage ; or une galerie d'art ne constitue pas un lieu de passage.

"I couldn't believe what I was looking at. I suddenly felt I could not stay in the gallery any longer. I realized I was red with embarrassment."

„Ich konnte es nicht fassen, was ich da vor mir sah. Ich merkte, dass ich keinen Augenblick länger in der Galerie bleiben konnte. Ich war vor Scham knallrot angelaufen."

« Je n'arrivais pas à croire à ce que je voyais. J'ai soudain eu la sensation que je ne pouvais pas rester dans cette galerie une minute de plus. Je me suis rendu compte que j'étais rouge de honte. »

NANSI CREER, HOUSEWIFE AND EGHAM JUSTICE OF THE PEACE

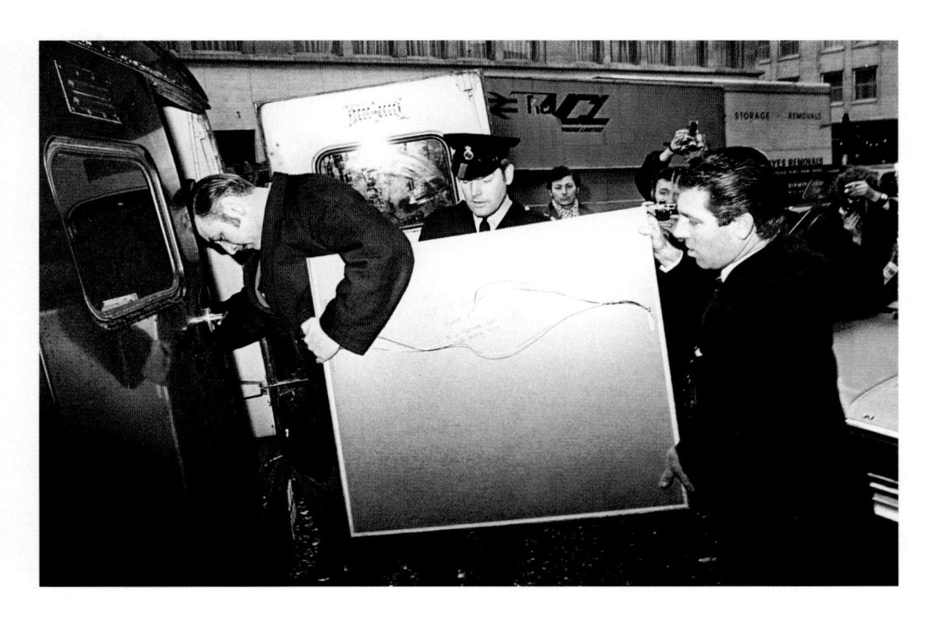

TUESDAY, JANUARY 27, 1970

Recorded in ten takes, with Lennon playing acoustic guitar, George Harrison on lead guitar, Plastic Ono Band regulars—Billy Preston, Klaus Voormann and Alan White—and Allen Klein and assorted clubgoers from London's Hatchetts club on backing vocals, Lennon's *Instant Karma! (We All Shine On)* is written, recorded and mixed in a session lasting nine hours from beginning to end. Phil Spector—who is in discussions to oversee final production on the Beatles' ***Let It Be***—produces.

John Lennons *Instant Karma! (We All Shine On)* wird innerhalb einer einzigen Session, die nicht mehr als neun Stunden dauert, geschrieben, aufgenommen und abgemischt. Bei der Aufnahme mit nur zehn Takes spielt John Lennon akustische Gitarre, George Harrison Leadgitarre, während die Mitglieder der Plastic Ono Band – Billy Preston, Klaus Voormann und Alan White – sowie Allen Klein und Clubbesucher des Londoner Hatchetts Clubs die Backingvocals singen. Produzent ist Phil Spector, der sich gerade in Gesprächen um die Leitung der Endproduktion des Beatles-Albums ***Let It Be*** befindet.

Enregistré en dix prises, avec Lennon à la guitare acoustique, George Harrison à la guitare lead, les habitués du Plastic Ono Band – Billy Preston, Klaus Voormann et Alan White –, Allen Klein et un groupe de fêtards du club londonien Hatchetts aux chœurs, le morceau de Lennon *Instant Karma! (We All Shine On)* est composé, enregistré et mixé au cours d'une unique session de neuf heures. Il est produit par Phil Spector – en pourparlers pour superviser la production finale de l'album ***Let It Be*** des Beatles.

WEDNESDAY, FEBRUARY 4, 1970

John and Yoko donate their recently-shorn hair for an auction in aid of the Black Power movement. They swap their mops for Muhammad Ali's blood-spattered boxing shorts with Black Power leader Michael X at his Black House in Holloway. (Despite pleas for clemency from Lennon, Michael X will be hanged in Trinidad for the murder of Joseph Skerritt in 1975.)

John und Yoko spenden ihre vor Kurzem abgeschnittenen Haare einer Auktion für die Black-Power-Bewegung. Sie tauschen ihre Mähnen gegen Muhammad Alis blutbespritzte Boxershorts, die sie vom Black-Power-Führer Michael X vor seinem Black House in Holloway in Empfang nehmen. (Trotz John Lennons Gnadengesuchen wird Michael X 1975 für den Mord an Joseph Skerritt in Trinidad gehängt.)

John et Yoko font don de leur chevelure fraîchement coupée à une vente aux enchères en soutien au mouvement du Black Power. Ils échangent leurs crinières hippie contre un short éclaboussé de sang de Mohammed Ali avec le dirigeant du Black Power Michael X, devant sa « Maison noire » de Holloway. (Malgré les appels à la clémence émis par Lennon, Michael X sera pendu à Trinidad en 1975 pour le meurtre de Joseph Skerritt.)

THURSDAY, FEBRUARY 12, 1970

Lennon becomes the first ex-Beatle to appear on BBC1-TV's "Top Of The Pops" as a solo artist, performing his new single, *Instant Karma! (We All Shine On)*. (The Beatles last appeared on the show in June 1966.)

John Lennon wird der erste Ex-Beatle, der als Solokünstler in „Top Of The Pops" auf BBC1 auftritt, wo er seine neue Single *Instant Karma! (We All Shine On)* vorstellt. (Die Beatles waren das letzte Mal im Juni 1966 in der Sendung zu sehen.)

Lennon est le premier ex-Beatle à participer en solo à l'émission « Top Of The Pops » de la BBC1 ; il chante son nouveau titre, *Instant Karma! (We All Shine On)*. (La dernière apparition des Beatles dans l'émission remonte à juin 1966.)

THURSDAY, APRIL 30, 1970

With John and Yoko having begun an intensive course of primal scream therapy under the guidance of its originator, Dr. Arthur Janov, they now fly to Los Angeles to study further at his Primal Institute in California. Renting a house in Bel Air, they will stay for four months.

John und Yoko haben mit einer intensiven Urschreitherapie unter Anleitung des Begründers Dr. Arthur Janov begonnen und fliegen nach Los Angeles, um das Studium an seinem Primal Institute in Kalifornien fortzusetzen. Sie mieten ein Haus in Bel Air und bleiben vier Monate.

John et Yoko ont commencé une thérapie par le « cri primal » sous l'égide du créateur de cette technique, le Dr Arthur Janov, et se rendent à Los Angeles pour approfondir leur initiation au Primal Institute de Californie. Pendant les quatre mois que dure leur séjour, ils louent une maison à Bel Air.

"John has made the universal statement.
I believe it will transform the world."

„John hat die Universalaussage gemacht. Ich bin überzeugt, dass sie die Welt verändern wird."

« John a prononcé des paroles universelles.
Je pense qu'elles vont changer le monde. »

ARTHUR JANOV

SATURDAY, SEPTEMBER 26, 1970

Returning from New York two days ago, Lennon begins recording at Abbey Road Studios with producer Phil Spector. The songs, already demoed in Los Angeles while Lennon was undergoing primal therapy treatment, will form the basis of his ***John Lennon/Plastic Ono Band*** album.

John Lennon ist zwei Tage zuvor aus New York nach London gekommen, wo er zusammen mit Phil Spector als Produzent mit Aufnahmen in den Abbey Road Studios beginnt. Die Songs, von denen John bereits in Los Angeles Demobänder angefertigt hat, während er sich dort der Primärtherapie unterzog, bilden die Basis für das Album ***John Lennon/Plastic Ono Band***.

Arrivé de New York deux jours plus tôt, Lennon entre en studio à Abbey Road avec le producteur Phil Spector. Les chansons, préparées pendant le séjour initiatique de Lennon à Los Angeles, serviront de base à son album ***John Lennon/Plastic Ono Band***.

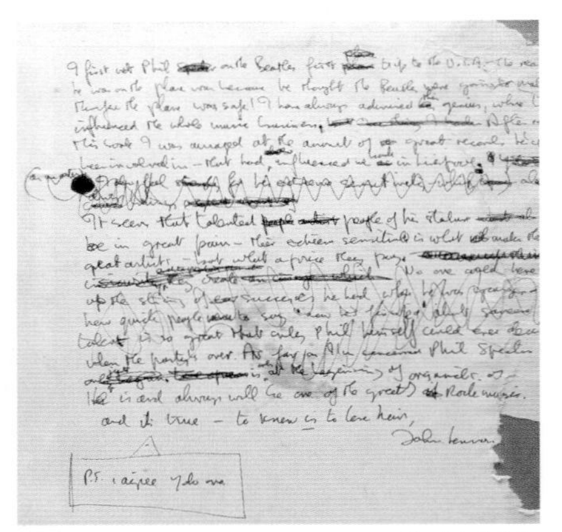

I first met Phil on the Beatles first trip to the U.S.A. – the reason he was on the plane was because he thought the Beatles were going to make it and therefore the plane was safe! I have always admired his genius, which influenced the whole music business. After this book I was amazed at the amount of great records he'd been involved in – that had influenced me in his [illegible]

[illegible]

It seems that talented people of his stature [illegible] be in great pain – their extreme sensitivity is what makes them great artists – but what a price they pay. [illegible] No one [illegible] up the string of successes he had when he was [illegible] how quickly people want to say [illegible] talent is so great that only Phil himself could ever [illegible] when the party's over. As far as I'm concerned Phil Spector is at the beginning of [illegible] He is and always will be one of the greats of Rock music.

and it's true – to know is to love him,

John Lennon

P.S. I agree Yoko ono

© Hard Rock Cafe

TUESDAY, DECEMBER 8, 1970

Lennon conducts an in-depth interview with Jann Wenner of **Rolling Stone** magazine at his Greenwich Village apartment. The interview will appear in the January 21 and February 4 editions of the magazine.

John Lennon führt in seinem Apartment in Greenwich Village ein langes Gespräch mit Jann Wenner von der Zeitschrift **Rolling Stone**. Das Interview erscheint in den Ausgaben vom 21. Januar und 4. Februar 1971.

Lennon accorde une longue interview à Jann Wenner, du magazine **Rolling Stone**, dans son appartement de Greenwich Village. Elle sera publiée en deux épisodes les 21 janvier et 4 février.

"A declaration that the partnership business carried on by the plaintiff and the defendants under the names of The Beatles & Co., and constituted by a deed of partnership dated 19 April 1967 and made between the parties hereto, ought to be dissolved and that accordingly the same be dissolved."

„Eine Erklärung, dass die Personengesellschaft, die vom Kläger und den Beklagten unter dem Namen The Beatles & Co. geführt wurde und am 19. April 1967 durch Abschluss eines Gesellschaftsvertrags zwischen den Parteien konstituiert wurde, aufgelöst werden soll."

« Nous déclarons par la présente que la collaboration commerciale qui unissait le plaignant et les accusés sous le nom de The Beatles & Co., constituée par un contrat de société daté du 19 avril 1967 établi entre les parties susmentionnées, se voit dissoute par la présente. »

THURSDAY, DECEMBER 31, 1970

Paul McCartney brings suit to dissolve The Beatles & Co. partnership in the High Court. The **Daily Mirror** had published a front-page story in April, headlined "Paul Is Quitting The Beatles." In an interview with Ray Connolly, McCartney had said "The Beatles have left the Beatles—but no one wants to say the party's over. John's in love with Yoko, and he's no longer in love with the other three of us." Two months into the Beatles High Court case, Lennon, Harrison and Starr will abandon their appeal from a court order brought by McCartney against them. Lord Justice Russell says their decision brought "tidings of great joy" to his court.

Paul McCartney erhebt Klage vor dem britischen High Court und verlangt die Auflösung der Beatles. Der **Daily Mirror** brachte bereits im April die Schlagzeile „Paul verlässt die Beatles". In einem Interview mit Ray Connolly hat Paul McCartney gesagt: „Die Beatles haben die Beatles verlassen – es will nur keiner zugeben, dass die Party vorbei ist. John liebt Yoko und hat für uns drei anderen keine Liebe mehr übrig." Nach zwei Monaten Gerichtsverhandlungen nehmen John Lennon, George Harrison und Ringo Starr ihren Widerspruch gegen die gerichtliche Anordnung zurück. Lordrichter Russell gibt bekannt, diese Entscheidung sei für sein Gericht „eine Botschaft großer Freude".

Paul McCartney engage un procès pour que l'entité juridique The Beatles & Co. soit dissoute. En avril, le **Daily Mirror** avait déjà publié en première page un article intitulé : « Paul quitte les Beatles ». Dans une interview accordée à Ray Connolly, McCartney déclarait : « Les Beatles ont quitté les Beatles – mais personne ne veut admettre que la fête est finie. John est amoureux de Yoko, et il n'est plus amoureux de nous trois. » Deux mois après le début de l'action en justice, Lennon, Harrison et Starr renoncent à faire appel contre McCartney. Le juge Russell déclare que leur décision a déclenché « une déferlante de joie » dans son tribunal.

SATURDAY, MAY 15, 1971

Further showcasing their avant-garde artistic bent, two short films by the Lennons premiere at the Filmmakers' Fortnight Festival, running concurrently with the Cannes Film Festival: "Apotheosis" and "The Fly." These are the latest in an ongoing collection of films made by the pair over the past three years.

Zwei avantgardistische Kurzfilme der Lennons haben beim Filmmakers' Fortnight Festival Premiere, das parallel zum Filmfestival in Cannes stattfindet: „Apotheosis" und „The Fly". Die beiden künstlerisch orientierten Filme sind Teil einer fortlaufenden Serie von Filmen, die das Paar im Laufe der vergangenen drei Jahre produziert hat.

Nouvelle étape sur leur trajectoire artistique d'avant-garde, les Lennon présentent deux courts métrages en avant-première de la Quinzaine des réalisateurs qui se tient parallèlement au Festival de Cannes : « Apotheosis » et « The Fly. » Ces deux films font partie d'une collection toujours croissante tournée par le couple depuis trois ans.

SUNDAY, JUNE 6, 1971

At the insistence of Andy Warhol, John and Yoko jam with Frank Zappa & the Mothers of Invention for the latter's encore at the Fillmore East in New York. The show—Lennon's first stage appearance since 1969—is recorded and subsequently included as one LP on his forthcoming double solo album, ***Sometime In New York City***. They perform *Well (Baby Please Don't Go)*, *Jamrag*, *Scumbag* and *Aü*. During their two-week stay in the city, the Lennons meet political radicals Abbie Hoffman and Jerry Rubin as well as musician David Peel.

Auf nachdrücklichen Wunsch Andy Warhols hin jammen John und Yoko mit Frank Zappa & the Mothers of Invention bei deren Zugabe im Fillmore East in New York. Das Konzert – John Lennons erster Bühnenauftritt seit 1969 – wird mitgeschnitten und die LP ist später Bestandteil des Doppel-Soloalbums ***Sometime In New York City***. Sie spielen *Well (Baby Please Don't Go)*, *Jamrag*, *Scumbag* und *Aü*. Während ihres zweiwöchigen New-York-Aufenthalts treffen sich die Lennons mit den Politaktivisten Abbie Hoffman und Jerry Rubin und mit dem Musiker David Peel.

Sur l'insistance d'Andy Warhol, John et Yoko se joignent à Frank Zappa & the Mothers of Invention pour les rappels, au Fillmore East à New York. Le concert – première apparition de Lennon sur scène depuis 1969 – est enregistré et constituera un des deux albums de sa prochaine production en solo, ***Sometime In New York City***. Ils jouent *Well (Baby Please Don't Go)*, *Jamrag*, *Scumbag* et *Aü*. Pendant les deux semaines qu'ils passent en ville, les Lennon rencontrent des figures du radicalisme politique comme Abbie Hoffman et Jerry Rubin, et le musicien David Peel.

"This is a song I used to sing when I was in the Cavern in Liverpool. I haven't done it since."

„Das hier ist ein Song, den ich gesungen habe, als ich im Cavern in Liverpool aufgetreten bin. Seitdem habe ich ihn nicht mehr gesungen."

« C'est une chanson que je chantais au Cavern de Liverpool. Je ne l'ai pas chantée depuis. »

JOHN LENNON

© Christie's

"The Ono-Lennon marriage brings together one of the most extraordinary representatives of popular culture in the history of the world. The results are sometimes puzzling and sometimes frustrating, but almost always provocative."

„Die Ono-Lennon-Ehe bringt einen der außergewöhnlichsten Repräsentanten der Popkultur weltweit hervor. Das Ergebnis ist manchmal rätselhaft und manchmal frustrierend, aber fast immer provokativ."

« Le mariage Ono-Lennon unit deux des représentants les plus extraordinaires de la culture populaire dans l'histoire du monde. Les résultats de cette rencontre sont parfois déroutants, parfois frustrants, mais presque toujours provocateurs. »

HIGH FIDELITY MAGAZINE

"This is an incredible Lennon album, an album that has already paled McCartney, Harrison and Starr into a living, but watercolor, backdrop ... It's the best album of the year, and for me it's the best album he's done, with anything, or with anyone, at any time."

„Es ist ein unglaubliches Lennon-Album, ein Album, das McCartney, Harrison und Starr in den Schatten stellt und sie jetzt schon zu einem lebenden, aber blassen Hintergrund werden lässt ... Es ist das beste Album des Jahres, für mich das beste Album, das er je gemacht hat."

« Lennon signe là un album incroyable, un album qui relègue déjà McCartney, Harrison et Starr à l'arrière-plan. [...] C'est le meilleur album de l'année, et pour moi c'est le meilleur qu'il ait jamais sorti, toutes catégories confondues. »

ROY HOLLINGWORTH, MELODY MAKER

WEDNESDAY, JUNE 23, 1971

Work begins on a new album, which will emerge as ***Imagine***, using an eight-track studio installed at Tittenhurst Park. The sessions will come to an end on July 2, at which point John and Yoko will fly to New York to add sweetening at the Record Plant. Containing two thinly-veiled attacks on Paul McCartney on *Crippled Inside* and *How Do You Sleep?*, the set features the backing unit of Nicky Hopkins (piano), Jim Keltner and Alan White (drums), and Klaus Voormann (bass). The (white) piano-led, utopian-themed title ballad, *Imagine*, will become revered as the artist's signature solo moment.

Die Lennons haben in ihrer Villa in Tittenhurst Park ein Achtspur-Tonstudio eingerichtet, in dem sie mit der Arbeit an einem neuen Album beginnen, aus dem später ***Imagine*** wird. Die Sessions enden am 2. Juli, als John und Yoko nach New York fliegen, wo sie die Bänder im Record Plant weiterbearbeiten. Der Set enthält auch *Crippled Inside* und *How Do You Sleep?*, zwei kaum verschleierte Seitenhiebe gegen Paul McCartney. Mit im Studio sind Nicky Hopkins (Piano), Jim Keltner und Alan White (Drums) und Klaus Voormann (Bass). Die utopische Titelballade *Imagine* mit der Begleitung am (weißen) Klavier wird als der Höhepunkt von John Lennons Solokarriere Geschichte machen.

Lennon commence à travailler sur son prochain album, qui deviendra ***Imagine***, dans un studio huit-pistes installé à Tittenhurst Park. Les séances s'achèvent le 2 juillet, et John et Yoko retournent à New York pour peaufiner l'album chez Record Plant. Le disque, qui comporte deux titres teintés de reproche à l'égard de Paul McCartney (*Crippled Inside* et *How Do You Sleep?*), est réalisé avec Nicky Hopkins (piano), Jim Keltner et Alan White (batterie) et Klaus Voormann (basse). La ballade utopiste accompagnée au piano (blanc) qui donne son titre à l'album, *Imagine*, est considérée comme l'apogée de l'œuvre solo de Lennon.

SATURDAY, JULY 17, 1971

John and Yoko are guests on the fifth edition of the BBC1-TV's new late-night chat show, "Parkinson." Lennon intercepts and refutes host Michael Parkinson's question to Yoko. "Recently, another reason for people taking a dislike to you, is because you're known again through the newspapers, as the woman who broke up the Beatles." Lennon retorts: "That's not true. I tell you, people on the streets and kids do not dislike us. It's the media. I'm telling ya. We go on the streets and the lorry drivers wave, 'Hello John, hello Yoko', all that jazz, and I judge it by that. My records still sell well. Her records sell all right." Lennon adds: "The British press actually called her ugly. I've never seen that about any woman or man, even if the person is ugly."

John und Yoko sind bei der fünften Ausgabe der BBC1-Late-Night-Talkshow „Parkinson" zu Gast. John wehrt eine Frage des Moderators Michael Parkinson an Yoko ab: „In jüngster Zeit gab es einen weiteren Grund, warum die Leute Sie nicht leiden können – Sie wurden in den Zeitungen als die Frau bekannt, wegen der sich die Beatles aufgelöst haben." John Lennon kontert: „Das ist nicht wahr. Ich sage Ihnen: Die Leute auf der Straße und die jungen Leute können uns sehr wohl leiden. Es sind die Medien, ich sag's Ihnen. Wenn wir auf die Straße gehen, dann winken uns die Lkw-Fahrer zu: ‚Hallo, John, hallo, Yoko' und so weiter, das ist für mich das deutlichste Zeichen. Meine Platten verkaufen sich gut. Ihre Platten verkaufen sich auch nicht schlecht." John fügt hinzu: „In der britischen Presse hat man sie tatsächlich als hässlich bezeichnet. So etwas habe ich noch nie über jemanden gelesen, selbst wenn der Mann oder die Frau tatsächlich hässlich ist."

John et Yoko sont invités à la cinquième édition de l'émission « Parkinson », diffusée en fin de soirée sur BBC1. Lennon intervient pour répondre à une question que Michael Parkinson pose à Yoko : « Récemment, les gens ont eu une autre raison de ne pas vous apprécier, parce que les journaux vous présentent comme la femme qui a séparé les Beatles. » Lennon rétorque : « Ce n'est pas vrai. Je vous le dis, les gens de la rue, les enfants, ils ne nous détestent pas. Ce sont les médias. Je vous le dis. Nous marchons dans la rue et les routiers nous saluent de la main, les gens nous disent "Salut John, salut Yoko", et tout le bazar, et c'est là-dessus que je m'appuie. Mes disques se vendent encore très bien. Ses albums se vendent pas mal. » Et il ajoute : « La presse britannique l'a qualifiée d'horrible. Je n'ai jamais lu une telle remarque sur quelque homme ou femme que ce soit, même quand ils étaient effectivement horribles. »

*"We're going on the road next year—John and Yoko—
and we'll have a band. We'd like to come and do live performances."*

*„Nächstes Jahr gehen wir auf Tournee – John und Yoko –, mit einer Band. Wir würden gern
wiederkommen und Live-Auftritte machen."*

*« Nous partons sur les routes l'année prochaine – John et Yoko – et nous serons accompagnés
par un groupe. On aimerait vraiment faire des concerts et des performances en direct. »*

JOHN LENNON, DICK CAVETT SHOW, SEPTEMBER 11, 1971

TUESDAY, AUGUST 31, 1971

John and Yoko fly from London's Heathrow Airport. On their arrival in New York, they check in to the St. Regis Hotel. Lennon will never set foot on British soil again.

John und Yoko fliegen ab Heathrow Airport und verlassen London. Nach ihrer Ankunft in New York wohnen sie im St. Regis Hotel. John wird nie wieder britischen Boden betreten.

John et Yoko s'envolent de l'aéroport londonien de Heathrow. À leur arrivée à New York, ils s'installent à l'hôtel St Regis. Lennon ne reposera plus jamais le pied sur le sol britannique.

"In England I'm regarded as the guy who won the pools. She's regarded as the lucky Jap who married the guy who won the pools. In America we are both treated as artists."

„In England werde ich als der Typ gesehen, der sechs Richtige getippt hat. Sie wird als die Japanerin angesehen, die Schwein gehabt und den Typen abgekriegt hat, der sechs Richtige getippt hat. In Amerika werden wir beide wie Künstler behandelt."

« En Angleterre, on me considère comme le gars qui a touché le gros lot. Elle, on la considère comme la Japonaise veinarde qui a épousé le gars qui a touché le gros lot. En Amérique, on nous traite tous les deux comme des artistes. »

JOHN LENNON

SATURDAY, SEPTEMBER 11, 1971

John and Yoko appear on "The Dick Cavett Show," talking on a variety of subjects, including the breakup of the Beatles, the new album ***Imagine***, its accompanying film, Yoko's book **Grapefruit**, her film "Fly", John's film "Erection," Yoko's new single *Mrs. Lennon* and her first one-woman show at the Everson Museum of Art in Syracuse, New York.

John und Yoko treten in der „Dick Cavett Show", auf, wo sie über Themen wie die Auflösung der Beatles, das neue Album ***Imagine***, den Film dazu, Yokos Buch **Grapefruit**, ihren Film „Fly", Johns Film „Erection", Yokos neue Single *Mrs. Lennon* und ihre erste Einzelausstellung im Everson Museum of Art in Syracuse, New York, sprechen.

John et Yoko participent au « Dick Cavett Show », où ils évoquent divers sujets parmi lesquels la séparation des Beatles, le nouvel album ***Imagine***, le film qui l'accompagne, le livre de Yoko, **Grapefruit**, son film « Fly », le film de John « Erection », le nouveau 45 tours de Yoko *Mrs. Lennon*, et son premier « one-woman show » à l'Everson Museum of Art de Syracuse (État de New York).

"The English are famous eccentrics.
I'm just another one from a long line of eccentrics."

„Die Engländer sind berühmt für ihr exzentrisches Benehmen. Ich reihe mich ein in die lange Tradition exzentrischer Typen."

« Les Anglais sont connus pour être des excentriques. Je ne suis qu'un personnage de plus dans une longue lignée d'excentriques. »

JOHN LENNON, MELODY MAKER, OCTOBER 2, 1971

SATURDAY, OCTOBER 16, 1971

With Bob Dylan among their neighbors, John and Yoko move into an apartment at 105 Bank Street, Greenwich Village, owned by former Lovin' Spoonful drummer, Joe Butler. Two days ago, their appearance on WNET's "Free Time" caused controversy with 250 calls to the network complaining about the nudity seen in the show.

John und Yoko ziehen in die Bank Street 105 in Greenwich Village in eine Wohnung, die dem ehemaligen Drummer von Lovin' Spoonful Joe Butler gehört. Zu ihren Nachbarn zählt Bob Dylan. Ihr Erscheinen in der WNET-Sendung „Free Time" zwei Tage zuvor verursachte eine Menge Aufregung, 250 Anrufer beschwerten sich beim Sender über das gezeigte nackte Fleisch.

John et Yoko emménagent au 105 Bank Street, à Greenwich Village, non loin de chez Bob Dylan, dans un appartement appartenant au batteur des Lovin' Spoonful, Joe Butler. Deux jours plus tôt, leur passage dans l'émission « Free Time » de WNET a déclenché la polémique : 250 téléspectateurs ont appelé la chaîne pour se plaindre des scènes de nudité montrées pendant l'émission.

THURSDAY, OCTOBER 28, 1971

Sessions begin at the Record Plant on *Happy Xmas (War Is Over)*. Further recordings will take place on Sunday augmented by the 30-strong Harlem Community Choir, after which all the participants, including musicians Jim Keltner, Nicky Hopkins, Klaus Voormann and producer Phil Spector, will gather round a plastic Christmas tree for a group photo.

Sessions für *Happy Xmas (War Is Over)* beginnen im Record Plant. Am Sonntag finden mit Unterstützung des 30-köpfigen Harlem Community Choir weitere Aufnahmen statt. Hinterher versammeln sich alle Mitwirkenden, auch die Musiker Jim Keltner, Nicky Hopkins, Klaus Voormann und Produzent Phil Spector für ein Gruppenfoto um einen Plastikweihnachtsbaum.

L'enregistrement de *Happy Xmas (War Is Over)* débute chez Record Plant. Le dimanche suivant, les 30 chanteurs du Harlem Community Choir participent à une séance supplémentaire, à l'issue de laquelle tout le monde, y compris les musiciens Jim Keltner, Nicky Hopkins et Klaus Voormann et le producteur Phil Spector se rassemble autour d'un sapin de Noël en plastique pour une photo de groupe.

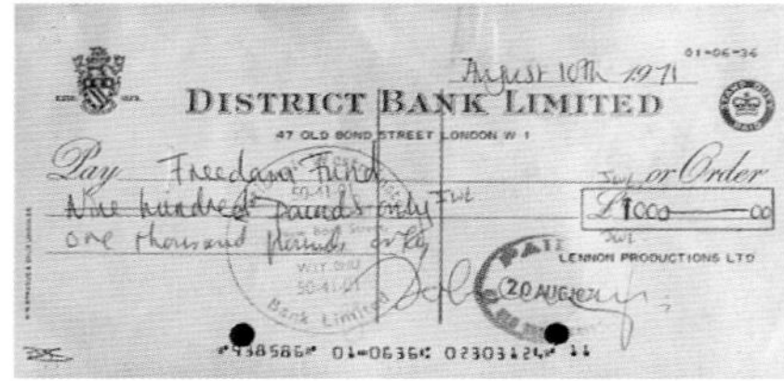

FRIDAY, DECEMBER 10, 1971

At the behest of Jerry Rubin, Lennon performs at Ann Arbor's Crisler Arena at the University of Michigan benefit show for imprisoned ex-MC5 manager and political activist, John Sinclair. The one-time leader of the Rainbow People's Party was jailed for 10 years following a conviction for attempting to sell two joints to an undercover cop. After a succession of political statements and performances from other musicians, Lennon will finally take the stage at 3:00 a.m. tomorrow morning, with FBI agents in the audience writing down the lyrics of his songs. Approximately 48 hours later, Sinclair will be released from prison.

Auf Drängen von Jerry Rubin spielt John Lennon bei einem Benefizkonzert für den inhaftierten Ex-MC5-Manager und Aktivisten John Sinclair in der Crisler Arena der University of Michigan in Ann Arbor. Der frühere Führer der Rainbow People's Party wurde zu zehn Jahren Haft verurteilt, nachdem er einem verdeckten Ermittler zwei Marihuana-Zigaretten verkaufen wollte. Nach einer langen Abfolge von politischen Reden und Musik geht Lennon endlich am nächsten Morgen um 3 Uhr auf die Bühne, während die FBI-Agenten im Publikum die Songtexte mitschreiben. Rund 48 Stunden später wird Sinclair aus dem Gefängnis entlassen.

À la demande de Jerry Rubin, Lennon se produit à la Ann Arbor's Crisler Arena de l'Université du Michigan pour un concert caritatif au profit de l'ex-manager des MC5 John Sinclair. L'ancien chef du Rainbow People's Party a été condamné à 10 ans de prison pour avoir tenté de vendre deux joints à un policier en civil. Après une série de déclarations politiques et de concerts d'autres artistes, Lennon finit par monter sur scène à trois heures du matin. Dans le public, des agents du FBI consignent les paroles de ses chansons. Environ 48 heures plus tard, Sinclair est libéré.

FRIDAY, DECEMBER 17, 1971

The day after taping an appearance on "The David Frost Show," the Lennons appear on stage at the Apollo Theatre in Harlem, New York, at a benefit concert for the wives of the victims of the Attica State Prison riot in September. John performs an acoustic version of *Imagine*. Becoming increasingly politically active, he had met with Chief Lion and the Onondaga Indian tribe in Syracuse in October and will attend the trial of the Harlem Six—the fourth trial of six teenagers held without bail since a murder in 1964—next month.

Die Lennons sind auf der Bühne des Apollo Theaters in Harlem, New York, bei einem Benefizkonzert für die Frauen der Opfer der Gefängnisrevolte im Attica State Prison im September zu sehen. John Lennon spielt *Imagine* in einer Version mit Akustikgitarre. Johns politisches Engagement nimmt weiter zu, im Oktober traf er sich in Syracuse mit Chief Lion und dem Indianerstamm der Onondaga, im kommenden Monat wird er dem Verfahren gegen die Harlem Six beiwohnen.

Après une apparition au « David Frost Show » la veille, les Lennon se produisent à l'Apollo Theatre de Harlem, à New York, lors d'un concert de soutien aux épouses des victimes de l'émeute de la prison d'Attica. Lennon chante une version acoustique d'*Imagine*. De plus en plus engagé, il a rencontré le chef indien Lion et la tribu Onondaga à Syracuse en octobre et assisté, un mois plus tard, au procès des « Six de Harlem » - la quatrième comparution de six adolescents accusés d'un meurtre commis en 1964 et emprisonnés depuis.

FRIDAY, FEBRUARY 4, 1972

William Timmons, assistant to President Nixon, receives a memo from South Carolina Senator Strom Thurmond, also copied to Attorney General John Mitchell. Thurmond claims Lennon is involved with a radical group planning concerts in various cities culminating in San Diego, where the Republican National Convention is due to be held. He writes "This appears to me to be an important matter, and I think it would be well for it to be considered at the highest level. As I can see, many headaches might be avoided if appropriate action be taken in time."

William Timmons, Assistent von Präsident Nixon, erhält ein Memorandum von Strom Thurmond, dem Senator South Carolinas, mit einer Kopie an den Justizminister John Mitchell. Thurmond behauptet darin, John Lennon sei Mitglied einer radikalen Vereinigung, die Konzerte in mehreren Städten und als Höhepunkt in San Diego plane, wo die Republican National Convention stattfinden wird. Er schreibt; „Ich halte dies für eine wichtige Angelegenheit, und glaube, dass es gut wäre, dies auf höchster Ebene zu behandeln. Soweit ich die Sache sehe, kann man sich viele Kopfschmerzen ersparen, wenn rechtzeitig angemessene Maßnahmen ergriffen werden."

William Timmons, un des assistants du Président Nixon, reçoit un rapport du sénateur de Caroline du Sud, Strom Thurmond, envoyé en copie au procureur général John Mitchell. Thurmond affirme que Lennon est engagé dans un groupe radical qui prévoit une tournée de concerts dans différentes villes, qui s'achèverait à San Diego pendant la convention du parti républicain. Il écrit : « Cette affaire me semble de la plus haute importance et je pense qu'il serait bon de la prendre en compte au plus haut niveau. De mon point de vue, de nombreuses migraines pourront être évitées si les décisions appropriées sont prises à temps. »

TUESDAY, FEBRUARY 15, 1972 TO FRIDAY, FEBRUARY 18, 1972

After appearing on yesterday's syndicated television chat program, "The Mike Douglas Show," John and Yoko begin a four-day run as guest hosts. They interview libertarian Ralph Nader and actor Louis Nye, while music is provided by the Chambers Brothers and the Lennons themselves, who perform *It's So Hard* with their new backing band, Elephant's Memory. An increasingly eclectic guest list through the rest of the week includes Jerry Rubin, Surgeon General Dr. Jesse Steinfeld, macrobiotic chef Hilary Redleak, Peace Corps leader Joseph Blatchfold, bio-rhythms musician David Rosenbloom, Chuck Berry—an erstwhile Lennon rock 'n' roll hero—singing *Johnny B Goode*, Bobby Seale, black activist Marsha Martin, medical researcher Donald Williams, and singer Vivian Reed.

John und Yoko waren am Vortag in der landesweit ausgestrahlten Talksendung „The Mike Douglas Show" zu Gast, in der sie nun vier Tage lang Gastgeber spielen. Sie führen Interviews mit dem Freidenker Ralph Nader und dem Schauspieler Louis Nye, Musik gibt es von den Chambers Brothers und den Lennons selbst, die zusammen mit ihrer neuen Band Elephant's Memory *It's So Hard* spielen. Auf der immer ausgefalleneren Gästeliste stehen im Laufe der Woche noch Jerry Rubin, Gesundheitsminister Dr. Jesse Steinfeld, die makrobiotische Köchin Hilary Redleak, Peace-Corps-Leiter Joseph Blatchfold und Biorhythmusmusiker David Rosenbloom. Chuck Berry – einer von Johns frühen Rock 'n' Roll-Helden – singt *Johnny B Goode*; Bobby Seale, die schwarze Aktivistin Marsha Martin, der Mediziner Donald Williams und die Sängerin Vivian Reed sind ebenfalls dabei.

Invités le lundi à l'émission de débat participative « The Mike Douglas Show », John et Yoko entament quatre jours de marathon télévisé. Ils interviewent le militant libertaire Ralph Nader et l'acteur Louis Nye, tandis que le programme musical est assuré par les Chambers Brothers et les Lennon, qui jouent *It's So Hard* avec leur nouveau groupe, Elephant's Memory. Sur la liste de plus en plus éclectique des invités du couple figurent Jerry Rubin, le docteur Jesse Steinfeld, ministre de la Santé, le chef macrobiotique Hilary Redleak, le commandant du Peace Corps Joseph Blatchfold, le musicien expert en biorythmes David Rosenbloom, Chuck Berry – une des idoles de toujours de Lennon, qui chante *Johnny B Goode* –, Bobby Seale, la militante de la cause noire Marsha Martin, le chercheur Donald Williams et la chanteuse Vivian Reed.

WEDNESDAY, MARCH 1, 1972

Lennon begins work on what will emerge as the double album, ***Some Time In New York City***. Recorded in 19 days, the first disc, featuring Elephant's Memory, is overtly political on causes ranging from Northern Ireland to the imprisonment of radicals Angela Davis and John Sinclair. The other LP comprises the June 6, 1971 Fillmore East concert appearance with the Mothers of Invention. The Beatles' song-publishing arm, Northern Songs, refuses to recognize some of Yoko's composer credits with Lennon, resulting in a delay of the British release.

John Lennon beginnt mit der Arbeit an dem Doppelalbum ***Some Time In New York City***. Die erste Platte wird innerhalb von 19 Tagen mit der Band Elephant's Memory aufgenommen und handelt von einer Vielzahl politischer Themen von Nordirland bis zur Verhaftung der radikalen Amerikaner Angela Davis und John Sinclair. Die zweite LP besteht aus einem Konzert vom 6. Juni 1971 im Fillmore East zusammen mit den Mothers of Invention. Northern Songs, der Musikverlag der Beatles, verweigert in einigen Fällen Yokos Anerkennung als Komponistin zusammen mit John, was zu einer Verzögerung bei der britischen Veröffentlichung führt.

Lennon commence à travailler sur ce qui deviendra le double album ***Some Time In New York City***. Enregistré en 19 jours, le premier disque, sur lequel officie Elephant's Memory, délivre un message politique clair sur des causes allant de l'Irlande du Nord à l'emprisonnement des militants radicaux Angela Davis et John Sinclair. L'autre disque est constitué de la participation au concert des Mothers of Invention le 6 juin 1971 au Fillmore East. La maison d'édition dépositaire des droits sur les chansons des Beatles, Northern Songs, refuse de reconnaître la participation de Yoko à la composition de plusieurs chansons de Lennon, ce qui retarde la sortie du double album en Grande-Bretagne.

"John Lennon has the guts to risk offending when really he still wants to be loved."

„John Lennon hat den Mut, die Leute vor den Kopf zu stoßen, obwohl er doch im Grunde immer noch geliebt werden will."

« John Lennon a le courage de prendre le risque de choquer alors que tout ce qu'il veut, c'est être aimé. »

MELODY MAKER REVIEW, OCTOBER 7, 1972

"In connection with your previous inquiry concerning the former member of the Beatles, John Lennon, I thought you would be interested in learning that the Immigration and Naturalization Service has served notice on him that he is to leave this country no later than March 15. You may be assured the information you previously furnished has been appropriately noted."

„In Zusammenhang mit Ihrer Anfrage bezüglich des ehemaligen Mitgliedes der Beatles, John Lennon, vermute ich, dass es Sie interessieren wird, dass der Immigration and Naturalization Service ihm bis zum 15. März Zeit gegeben hat, das Land zu verlassen. Ich darf Ihnen versichern, dass die zuvor von Ihnen übermittelten Informationen zur Kenntnis genommen wurden."

« Concernant votre précédente requête sur l'ancien Beatles John Lennon, j'ai pensé que vous seriez ravi d'apprendre que les services d'immigration et de naturalisation lui ont fait savoir qu'il doit quitter ce pays avant le 15 mars. Soyez-en assuré, les informations que vous nous avez fournies ont été prises en considération comme elles le devaient. »

WILLIAM TIMMONS' REPLY TO STROM THURMOND, MARCH 6, 1972

THURSDAY, MARCH 16, 1972

Ten days after the Immigration and Naturalization Services inexplicably canceled their visa extensions and served them with deportation orders (which are slipped under their front door), the Lennons lodge an appeal. Although the official line is that the decision has been made because of his 1968 conviction for drug possession, Lennon believes that it is politically motivated.

Zehn Tage nachdem die Einwanderungsbehörde die Visumsverlängerung der Lennons ohne Erklärung für ungültig erklärt und ihnen einen Abschiebungsbefehl zugestellt hat (der bei ihnen unter der Tür durchgesteckt wird), legen sie Berufung ein. Als offizielle Begründung wird John Lennons Verurteilung 1968 wegen Drogenbesitz angegeben, doch er hält das Vorgehen für politisch motiviert.

Dix jours après l'annulation sans motif de leurs extensions de visa par les services d'immigration américains, qui ont glissé leurs avis d'expulsion sous leur porte d'entrée, les Lennon font appel. Le prétexte officiel est la condamnation prononcée contre Lennon pour possession de drogues en 1968, mais il est convaincu que la raison réelle de ce revirement est politique.

SATURDAY, APRIL 22, 1972

John and Yoko speak at a National Peace Coalition Rally in the rain at Duffy Square in New York. The crowd sings *Give Peace A Chance*.

John und Yoko sind Sprecher bei der verregneten Demonstration der National Peace Coalition auf dem Duffy Square in New York. Die Teilnehmer singen *Give Peace A Chance*.

John et Yoko prennent la parole sous la pluie au National Peace Coalition Rally, sur Duffy Square, à New York. La foule entonne *Give Peace A Chance*.

FRIDAY, APRIL 28, 1972

A press conference is held at the National Press Club in Washington, DC to announce the formation of the National Committee for John and Yoko. Calling the deportation proceedings "a grave injustice," New York Mayor, John V. Lindsay, in a letter to the Commissioner of the INS, requests that the couple be granted resident alien status.

Im National Press Club in Washington, D.C. findet eine Pressekonferenz statt, auf der die Bildung eines nationalen Komitees für John und Yoko bekannt gegeben wird. Der New Yorker Bürgermeister John V. Lindsay nennt das Abschiebungsverfahren in einem Brief an den Bevollmächtigten der Einwanderungsbehörde „völlig ungerechtfertigt" und bittet darum, dem Paar eine permanente Aufenthaltserlaubnis zu erteilen.

Une conférence de presse est organisée au National Press Club de Washington pour annoncer la formation du Comité national pour John et Yoko. Dans une lettre adressée au commissaire général de l'INS (service de l'immigration et des naturalisations), le maire de New York John V. Lindsay qualifie la procédure d'expulsion de « grave injustice » et demande à ce qu'un statut de résident étranger soit accordé au couple.

TUESDAY, MAY 2, 1972

Judge Bernard J. Lasker rules in Federal Court that the INS must hold a hearing on the Lennons' defense motion that they should be classified as "aliens of distinguished merit and ability" before they can hold a deportation hearing.

Richter Bernard J. Lasker urteilt vor dem Bundesgericht, dass die Einwanderungsbehörde vor der Durchführung eines Abschiebungsverfahren eine Anhörung über das Ersuchen durchführen muss, in dem die Lennons ein VIP-Visum für „Ausländer mit besonderen Fähigkeiten und Verdiensten" beantragt haben.

Le juge fédéral Bernard J. Lasker estime que l'INS doit tenir une audience sur la requête déposée par les Lennon, qui demandent à être considérés comme des « non-ressortissants distingués pour leur mérite et leurs compétences », avant d'envisager une procédure d'expulsion.

"If John Lennon were a painting, he would be hanging in the Metropolitan Museum."

„Wenn John Lennon ein Gemälde wäre, würde er im Metropolitan Museum hängen."

« Si John Lennon était une peinture, il serait accroché au Metropolitan Museum. »

THOMAS HOVING, DIRECTOR OF THE METROPOLITAN MUSEUM OF ART

"John Lennon should quit trying to make points with the American public, and do his own thing, like go back to England."

„John Lennon sollte endlich aufhören, die amerikanische Öffentlichkeit von seinen Ansichten zu überzeugen, und sich lieber um seine eigenen Angelegenheiten kümmern. Warum geht er nicht zurück nach England?"

« John Lennon devrait cesser d'essayer de marquer des points auprès du public américain et vaquer à ses occupations : retourner en Angleterre, par exemple. »

KIP PARKER, ACME MUSIC CO., MINNEAPOLIS

THURSDAY, MAY 11, 1972

Making their second appearance on "The Dick Cavett Show," John and Yoko claim their telephone conversations are being taped and that he is being followed by United States government agents. They also perform *Woman Is The Nigger Of The World*, despite ABC-TV bosses' objections.

John und Yoko sind zum zweiten Mal in der „Dick Cavett Show" zu Gast, in der John berichtet, ihre Telefongespräche würden mitgeschnitten und er würde von Agenten der amerikanischen Regierung verfolgt. Sie singen *Woman Is The Nigger Of The World*, trotz aller Einwände der Bosse von ABC-TV.

Lors de leur deuxième participation au « Dick Cavett Show », John et Yoko déclarent que leurs conversations téléphoniques sont enregistrées et qu'ils sont suivis par des agents gouvernementaux américains. Ils chantent aussi *Woman Is The Nigger Of The World*, malgré les objections des huiles d'ABC.

TUESDAY, JULY 4, 1972

The former British Ambassador to the United States, William David Ormsby-Gore, Lord Harlech, writes "As a life-long friend of the United States I reject the suggestion that the most powerful democratic country in the world, whose constitution is based on individual freedom and human rights could believe for one moment that it might be subverted by the presence of a single young artist ... Lennon has consistently made public his strongly held views in favor of non-violence and peace, and he has demonstrated in his works and in his life his compassion and concern for his fellow man."

Der ehemalige britische Botschafter in den Vereinigten Staaten, William David Ormsby-Gore, Lord Harlech, schreibt: „Ich bin mein ganzes Leben lang ein Freund der Vereinigten Staaten gewesen und lehne die Vorstellung ab, dass der mächtigste demokratische Staat der Welt, dessen Verfassung auf der Freiheit des Einzelnen und den Menschenrechten begründet ist, auch nur einen Augenblick lang glauben kann, dass ein einziger junger Künstler ihn untergraben könnte ... Lennon hat seine starken Überzeugungen für Gewaltlosigkeit und Frieden stets öffentlich geäußert und in seinem Leben und Werk Mitgefühl und Sorge für seine Mitmenschen demonstriert."

L'ancien ambassadeur britannique aux États-Unis William David Ormsby-Gore, Lord Harlech, écrit : « En tant qu'ami de toujours des États-Unis, je refuse de croire que la plus puissante démocratie du monde, dont la constitution est fondée sur la liberté individuelle et les droits de l'homme, puisse se sentir un instant menacée par la présence d'un seul jeune artiste. [...] Lennon a fait entendre haut et fort ses opinions les plus sincères en faveur de la non-violence et de la paix, et il a démontré dans son œuvre comme dans sa vie sa compassion et son intérêt pour son prochain. »

WEDNESDAY, AUGUST 30, 1972

John and Yoko headline two concerts at New York's Madison Square Garden, as part of "One To One," a day-long series of events to raise money and awareness for the Willowbrook School for Children, brought to the public's attention by a searing "Eyewitness News" TV report by Geraldo Rivera about conditions at the school for retarded children. John and Yoko, who prior to the concerts purchase $60,000 worth of tickets, distributing them to volunteer fundraisers, are joined on stage by fellow performers Stevie Wonder and Roberta Flack for the *Give Peace A Chance* finale.

John und Yoko sind die Headliner bei zwei Konzerten im New Yorker Madison Square Garden, ein Teil von „One To One", einer eintägigen Serie von Benefiz-Events für die Willowbrook School for Children. Die Öffentlichkeit ist auf die Zustände an dieser Schule für geistig behinderte Kinder durch eine Fernsehreportage von Geraldo Rivera in den „Eyewitness News" aufmerksam gemacht worden. John und Yoko haben Vorverkaufskarten im Wert von 60.000 Dollar gekauft und an die freiwilligen Helfer verteilt. Zum Finale gesellen sich Stevie Wonder und Roberta Flack bei *Give Peace A Chance* zu ihnen auf die Bühne.

John et Yoko figurent en tête d'affiche de deux concerts au Madison Square Garden de New York dans le cadre du festival « One To One » organisé pour lever des fonds et informer le public sur l'école Willowbrook. L'émission « Eyewitness News » a récemment diffusé un reportage sans concession de Geraldo Rivera sur les conditions dans lesquelles sont accueillis les enfants retardés dans cette école. John et Yoko, qui ont acheté pour 60 000 dollars de billets pour les bénévoles de l'association, sont rejoints sur scène par Stevie Wonder et Roberta Flack pour *Give Peace A Chance*, qui conclut le festival.

FRIDAY, MARCH 23, 1973

Lennon is ordered to leave the United States within 60 days in a ruling from Judge Ira Fieldsteel, who also grants Yoko permanent residency. This begins a new round of litigation and applications to gain the necessary "green card" which will enable him to remain in the country by his lawyer Leon Wildes.

Richter Ira Fieldsteel fällt das Urteil, dass John Lennon innerhalb von 60 Tagen die USA verlassen muss; Yoko erhält eine Aufenthaltserlaubnis. Daraufhin wird von Johns Anwalt Leon Wildes eine neue Prozessrunde eingeläutet, in der John Lennon sich um die „Green Card“ bemüht, mit der er dauerhaft im Land bleiben kann.

Lennon reçoit l'ordre de quitter les États-Unis dans les 60 jours en vertu d'une décision du juge Ira Fieldsteel, qui accorde en même temps le statut de résident permanent à Yoko. Ce verdict provoque une nouvelle série de litiges et de plaintes pour que Lennon, défendu par son avocat Leon Wildes, reçoive la « carte verte » qui lui permettrait de rester dans le pays.

"Having just celebrated our fourth wedding anniversary, we are not prepared to sleep in separate beds. Peace and love, John and Yoko."

„Wir haben gerade unseren vierten Hochzeitstag gefeiert und sind nicht bereit, in getrennten Betten zu schlafen. Liebe und Frieden, John und Yoko.“

« Nous venons de fêter nos quatre ans de mariage, et nous ne sommes pas prêts à faire chambre à part. Paix et amour. John et Yoko. »

JOHN & YOKO LENNON

WEDNESDAY, MARCH 28, 1973

The **Wall Street Journal** publishes an editorial castigating the INS for its action against the Lennons. "We've seldom considered ourselves apologists for the counterculture, but we really do think the laws have created an intolerable situation with regard to John Lennon and his wife Yoko Ono ... Further, we submit, if the law does not reflect the human equities, it is the law that needs to be changed."

Die Zeitung **Wall Street Journal** veröffentlicht einen Leitartikel, in dem sie die Einwanderungsbehörde für ihr Verfahren gegen die Lennons kritisiert. „Wir haben uns nur selten als Fürsprecher der Untergrundkultur angesehen, aber wir sind überzeugt, dass die Gesetzeshüter für John Lennon und Frau Yoko Ono eine unerträgliche Situation geschaffen haben ... Wenn das Gesetz keine Rücksicht auf menschliche Gerechtigkeit nimmt, dann geben wir zu bedenken, dass vielleicht das Gesetz geändert werden muss."

Le **Wall Street Journal** publie un éditorial virulent contre les Services de l'immigration : « Nous nous sommes rarement considérés comme des apologistes de la contre-culture, mais nous pensons vraiment que les lois mettent John Lennon et son épouse Yoko Ono dans une situation intolérable. [...] De plus, nous estimons que si la loi ne reflète pas l'équité entre les hommes, c'est la loi qui doit être changée. »

SUNDAY, APRIL 1, 1973

John and Yoko, and Leon Wildes, hold a press conference at the New York Bar Association to announce Nutopia Day. They wave the national flag—a tissue.

John und Yoko und Leon Wildes halten eine Pressekonferenz in der New Yorker Anwaltskammer ab und verkünden Nutopia Day.

John et Yoko, soutenus par Leon Wildes, tiennent une conférence de presse à la New York Bar Association pour annoncer la création de la communauté politique conceptuelle Nutopia.

"Declaration of Nutopia. We announce the birth of a conceptual country, Nutopia. Citizenship of the country can be obtained by declaration of your awareness of Nutopia. Nutopia has no land, no boundaries, no passports, only people. Nutopia has no laws other than cosmic. All people of Nutopia are ambassadors of the country. As two ambassadors of Nutopia, we ask for diplomatic immunity and recognition in the United Nations of our country and its people. John Ono Lennon, Yoko Ono Lennon, Nutopian Embassy, One White Street. New York, N.Y. 10013, April 1st, 1973."

„Erklärung von Nutopia. Wir verkünden die Geburt eines konzeptionellen Staates, Nutopia. Die Staatsbürgerschaft des Landes kann durch Erklärung des Bewusstseins von Nutopia erworben werden. Nutopia besitzt kein Land, keine Grenzen, keine Reisepässe, nur Menschen. Nutopia kennt keine Gesetze außer den kosmischen. Alle Bürger Nutopias sind Botschafter des Landes. Als zwei Botschafter von Nutopia ersuchen wir um diplomatische Immunität und Anerkennung unseres Landes und seiner Bürger durch die Vereinten Nationen. John Lennon, Yoko Ono Lennon, Nutopische Botschaft, 1 White Street, New York NY 10013, 1. April 1973."

« Fondation de Nutopia. Nous annonçons la naissance d'un pays conceptuel, Nutopia. Pour devenir citoyen de ce pays, il suffit d'en avoir connaissance. Nutopia n'a ni territoire, ni frontières, ni passeports, seulement un peuple. Nutopia n'a pas d'autre loi que cosmique. Tous les citoyens de Nutopia sont les ambassadeurs du pays. En tant qu'ambassadeurs de Nutopia, nous demandons l'immunité diplomatique et la reconnaissance de notre pays et de son peuple par les Nations-Unies. John Ono Lennon, Yoko Ono Lennon, Ambassade Nutopienne, 1, rue blanche, New York, N.Y. 10013, 1er avril 1973. »

APRIL 1973

John and Yoko move from their Greenwich Village apartment into the Dakota Building on New York's Upper West Side at 1, West 72nd Street. They bought the 12-room apartment from film actor, Robert Ryan.

John und Yoko ziehen aus ihrer Wohnung in Greenwich Village in das Dakota Building in der Upper West Side, West 72nd Street 1. Sie haben das 12-Zimmer-Apartment von dem Schauspieler Robert Ryan gekauft.

John et Yoko quittent leur appartement de Greenwich Village pour l'immeuble Dakota, dans l'Upper West Side, au 1 de la 72e rue Ouest. Ils ont racheté son appartement de 12 pièces à l'acteur Robert Ryan.

THURSDAY, JUNE 28, 1973

John and Yoko take part in a demonstration outside the South Vietnamese Embassy in Washington, DC. While in the capital, they also attend the Watergate hearings.

John und Yoko nehmen an einer Demonstration vor der südvietnamesischen Botschaft in Washington, D.C., teil. Solange sie in der Hauptstadt sind, besuchen sie auch die Anhörungen zum Watergate-Skandal.

John et Yoko participent à une manifestation devant l'ambassade du Sud-Vietnam à Washington. Ils profitent aussi de leur présence dans la capitale pour assister aux audiences du Watergate.

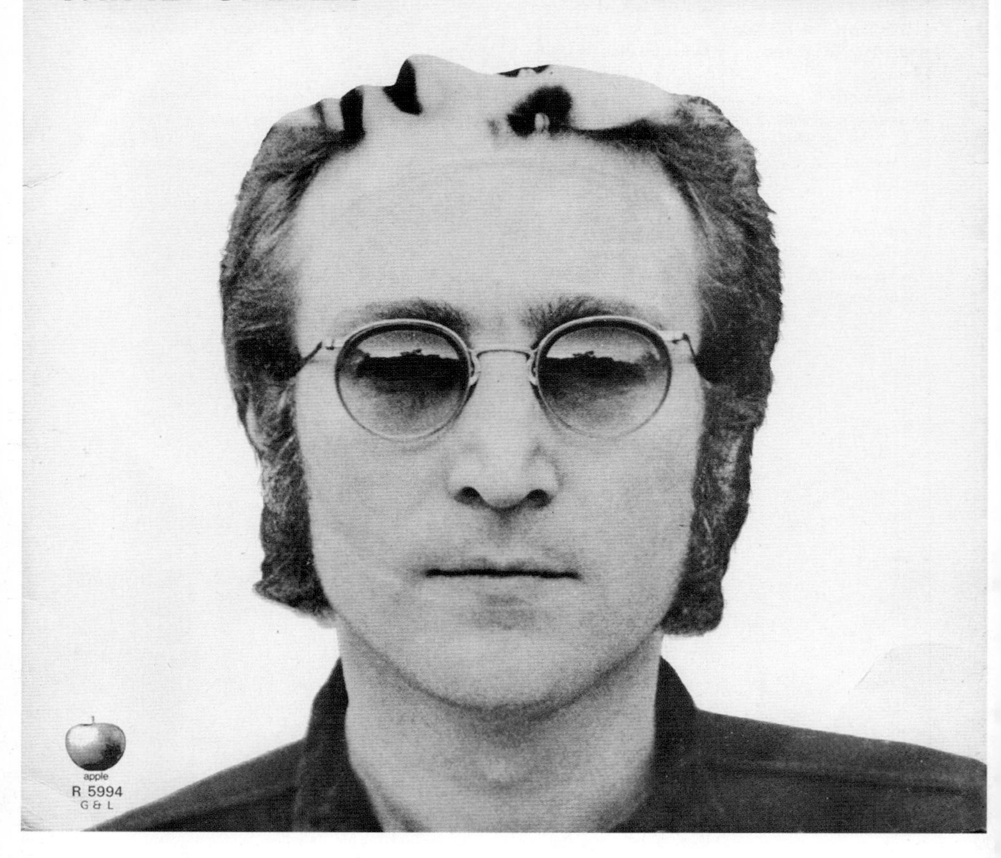

WEDNESDAY, JULY 4, 1973

Three days after Yoko began work on her third solo album at the Record Plant in New York, John does likewise, beginning a series of new sessions for what will evolve into the **Mind Games** album.

Drei Tage nachdem Yoko mit der Arbeit an ihrem dritten Soloalbum begonnen hat, geht John ebenfalls ins Record-Plant-Studio in New York. Aus seinen Sessions entwickelt sich das Album **Mind Games**.

Alors que Yoko travaille depuis trois jours sur son troisième album solo chez Record Plant, à New York, John retourne aussi en studio pour enregistrer ce qui deviendra l'album **Mind Games**.

TUESDAY, SEPTEMBER 18, 1973

Lennon moves out of the couple's Dakota apartment, before heading off to Los Angeles, where he will embark on a self-described 16-month long "Lost Weekend." At Yoko's suggestion he will spend his time with their personal assistant, May Pang. After initially staying at record producer, Lou Adler's home, he will move to a rented Santa Monica beach house.

John Lennon zieht aus der gemeinsamen Wohnung im Dakota Building aus und geht nach Los Angeles, zu einem „Lost Weekend", wie er es selbst nennt, das sechzehn Monate dauert. Auf Yokos Anregung verbringt er die Zeit mit der gemeinsamen Privatassistentin May Pang. Anfangs wohnt er im Haus des Musikproduzenten Lou Adler und zieht dann in ein gemietetes Haus am Santa Monica Beach.

Lennon quitte l'appartement du Dakota et s'envole pour Los Angeles, où il va vivre une parenthèse de 16 mois appelée son « week-end perdu » avec, comme l'a suggéré Yoko, leur assistante personnelle May Pang. Ils s'installent d'abord chez le producteur de disques Lou Adler, puis louent une maison sur la plage de Santa Monica.

"I can't say 'be happy' because I know there is no such thing. You're up and you're down ... I'm a complete neurotic, but I've just got to swing with it a bit more like when I was younger."

„Ich kann nicht sagen: ‚Sei doch einfach glücklich', weil ich weiß, dass es so etwas nicht gibt. Mal ist man oben, dann wieder unten ... Ich bin immer schon völlig neurotisch gewesen, aber als ich jünger war, hat es mir nicht so viel ausgemacht."

« Je ne peux pas dire "soyez heureux" parce que je sais que ça n'existe pas. Il y a des hauts et des bas... Je suis un névrosé complet, mais il me suffit de swinguer un peu plus avec la vie, comme quand j'étais plus jeune. »

JOHN LENNON, LOS ANGELES TIMES, DECEMBER 30, 1973

WEDNESDAY, OCTOBER 24, 1973

Having recently begun recording a series of rock 'n' roll classics, including *Sweet Little Sixteen, Bony Maronie* and *That'll Be The Day*, with Phil Spector in Los Angeles, Lennon begins a new round of litigation against the United States government, accusing it of illegal surveillance and wire tapping his telephone and that of his attorney, Leon Wildes—activity which has undermined the likelihood of him receiving a fair deportation trial.

John Lennon hat angefangen, mit Phil Spector in Los Angeles eine Reihe von Rock 'n' Roll-Klassikern aufzunehmen, u. a *Sweet Little Sixteen, Bony Maronie* und *That'll Be The Day*. Gleichzeitig beginnt John Lennon eine neue Prozessrunde gegen die amerikanische Regierung, die er beschuldigt, ihn und seinen Anwalt Leon Wildes illegal zu bespitzeln und abzuhören. Dadurch wird seiner Argumentation nach ein faires Abschiebungsverfahren praktisch unmöglich gemacht.

Alors qu'il a commencé l'enregistrement d'une série de classiques du rock 'n' roll comme *Sweet Little Sixteen, Bony Maronie* et *That'll Be The Day* avec Phil Spector à Los Angeles, Lennon se lance dans une nouvelle bagarre judiciaire contre le gouvernement américain, qu'il accuse de surveillance et d'écoutes illégales de sa ligne téléphonique et de celle de son avocat, Leon Wildes - des pratiques qui l'auraient empêché de bénéficier d'un procès équitable.

TUESDAY, MARCH 12, 1974

An inebriated Lennon is forcibly removed in the early hours (of tomorrow) from the Troubadour club in Los Angeles with drinking pal Harry Nilsson after hurling insults at the performing Smothers Brothers, punching their manager Ken Fritz and a cocktail waitress. The following day they send flowers with a note of apology ("To Tom and Dick. Please accept these flowers as a gesture of peace. We humbly apologize for our bad manners. Love and Tears, John and Harry").

Der betrunkene John Lennon wird zusammen mit Zechkumpan Harry Nilsson in den frühen Morgenstunden des 13. März aus dem Troubadour Club in Los Angeles geworfen, nachdem er die auf der Bühne stehenden Smothers Brothers lautstark beschimpft und ihren Manager Ken Fritz und eine Cocktailkellnerin geschlagen hat. Am nächsten Tag schicken sie Blumen und eine Entschuldigung („An Tom und Dick. Bitte nehmt diese Blumen als Geste der Versöhnung an. Wir entschuldigen uns untertänigst für unser schlechtes Benehmen. Mit Liebe und Tränen, John und Harry.")

Lennon, passablement ivre, est sorti par la force du Troubadour de Los Angeles aux premières heures du matin (le 13) avec son compère de boisson Harry Nilsson, après avoir hurlé des insultes pendant le set des Smothers Brothers et frappé leur manager Ken Fritz et une serveuse. Le lendemain, ils envoient des fleurs et un mot d'excuses (« Pour Tom et Dick. Veuillez accepter ces fleurs comme un geste de paix. Nous vous prions humblement d'excuser nos mauvaises manières. Amour et Larmes, John et Harry »).

"We sure brought out the screwballs tonight."

„Wir scheinen heute Nacht ja wirklich die Spinner angelockt zu haben."

« On a fait sortir les fêlés ce soir, ça c'est sûr. »

TOM SMOTHERS

THURSDAY, MARCH 28, 1974

Production on Nilsson's ***Pussycats***, with Lennon at the helm, begins at Burbank Studios. During the evening, Paul and Linda McCartney drop in on the sessions. Lennon and Nilsson will complete the album at the Record Plant in New York next month.

John Lennon ist der Produzent des Nilsson-Albums ***Pussycats***, das in den Burbank Studios aufgenommen wird. Am Abend schauen Paul und Linda McCartney bei den Sessions vorbei. Lennon und Nilsson stellen das Album einen Monat später im Record Plant in New York fertig.

La production de l'album de Nilsson, ***Pussycats***, chapeautée par Lennon, commence aux studios Burbank. Dans la soirée, Paul et Linda McCartney passent participer aux séances. Lennon et Nilsson achèveront l'album chez Record Plant, à New York, le mois suivant.

"What I'm back to is believing in everything until it's disproved."

„Ich bin jetzt wieder an dem Punkt, an dem ich alles glaube, bis es widerlegt worden ist."

« Je suis revenu à l'idée que tout est possible tant qu'on n'a pas prouvé le contraire. »

JOHN LENNON, CRAWDADDY, MARCH 1974

MONDAY, JUNE 17, 1974

Following his return to New York at the end of April and a move into the Pierre Hotel on 5th Avenue with May Pang, Lennon begins recording his ***Walls And Bridges*** project, which will include a duet with Elton John on *Whatever Gets You Through The Night* (his first United States No. 1 single). (On Friday, Lennon is informed by Al Coury, Capitol Records' head of promotions in Los Angeles, that he has recovered the tapes of the unfinished ***Rock 'n' Roll*** album, though not before handing over $90,000 to Phil Spector.)

John Lennon ist Ende April nach New York zurückgekehrt, wo er zusammen mit May Pang im Pierre Hotel an der 5th Avenue wohnt, und beginnt mit den Aufnahmen zu seinem Projekt ***Walls And Bridges***, zu dem auch ein Duett mit Elton John, *Whatever Gets You Through The Night* (seine erste Single auf Platz eins der US-Charts), gehört. Am Freitag erhält John die Nachricht von Al Coury, dem Werbeleiter von Capitol Records in Los Angeles, er habe die Bänder des unfertigen Albums ***Rock 'n' Roll*** zurückbekommen, allerdings erst nachdem er Phil Spector dafür 90.000 Dollar ausgehändigt habe.)

Revenu à New York fin avril pour s'installer au Pierre Hotel, sur la 5e Avenue, avec May Pang, Lennon entame l'enregistrement de son projet ***Walls And Bridges***, qui contient un duo avec Elton John sur *Whatever Gets You Through The Night* (son premier titre classé premier des ventes américaines). (Le vendredi, Lennon apprend par Al Coury, le responsable de la promotion chez Capitol Records à Los Angeles, qu'il a récupéré les bandes de l'album inachevé ***Rock 'n' Roll*** – non sans avoir donné 90 000 dollars à Phil Spector.)

"Yes, I know what you're thinking. I'm as crazy as my publicity always said I was? But no. Listen. This is true."

„Ja, ich weiß, was Sie denken: Ich bin so verrückt, wie ich von der Presse immer geschildert werde? Nein, hören Sie zu. Das ist wirklich wahr."

« Oui, je sais ce que vous pensez. Je suis aussi dingue que la publicité faite autour de moi l'a toujours prétendu ? Mais non. Écoutez. C'est la vérité. »

JOHN LENNON, MELODY MAKER, SEPTEMBER 14, 1974

SATURDAY AUGUST 31, 1974

One week after reporting a UFO sighting while standing naked on the roof of his apartment block, Lennon testifies in Federal Court that officials of the Nixon administration sought to deport him because of his anti-war rhetoric and particularly the suspicion he was involved in a plan to disrupt the Republican National Convention in San Diego. (Only last month, he had been given two months to leave the country.)

Eine Woche nachdem er nackt auf dem Dach seines Wohnblocks gestanden und ein UFO gesichtet hat, sagt John Lennon vor dem Bundesgericht aus, dass Mitglieder der Nixon-Regierung ihn wegen seiner Aussagen gegen den Krieg und besonders wegen des Verdachts, er sei Teil eines Komplotts zur Störung der Republican National Convention in San Diego, des Landes verweisen wollen. (Im Vormonat hatte man ihn wieder aufgefordert, die USA innerhalb von zwei Monaten zu verlassen.)

Après avoir raconté, une semaine plus tôt, qu'il a vu un OVNI alors qu'il se tenait nu sur le toit de son immeuble, Lennon témoigne devant la cour fédérale et affirme que des responsables de l'administration Nixon ont cherché à l'expulser en raison de son engagement contre la guerre, et en particulier parce qu'ils le soupçonnaient de vouloir perturber la convention républicaine de San Diego. (Le mois précédent, les autorités lui ont donné deux mois pour quitter le pays.)

MONDAY, OCTOBER 21, 1974

Lennon resumes work on the ***Rock 'n' Roll*** album, spending most of the next four days recording new vocals over the backing tracks from the earlier sessions. In the end, only four tracks from the sessions with Phil Spector will be retained.

John Lennon setzt seine Arbeit an dem ***Rock 'n' Roll***-Album fort und verbringt die nächsten vier Tage mit der Aufnahme von neuem Gesang für die Backingtracks aus den früheren Sessions. Am Ende bleiben nur vier Stücke aus den Aufnahmen mit Phil Spector übrig.

Lennon reprend le travail sur son album ***Rock 'n' Roll***, et passe le plus clair des quatre jours suivants à enregistrer de nouvelles voix sur les morceaux instrumentaux dont il dispose déjà. Le disque ne comptera finalement que quatre titres issus des séances d'enregistrement avec Phil Spector.

THURSDAY, NOVEMBER 28, 1974

Introduced by Elton John with the words "As it's Thanksgiving, we thought we'd give you a special present. So here's something to give thanks for," Lennon makes what will be his final concert appearance, at Madison Square Garden, joining Elton for three songs: *Whatever Gets You Through The Night*, *Lucy In The Sky With Diamonds* and *I Saw Her Standing There*. Following the gig, he reunites with Yoko backstage.

Elton John stellt John Lennon mit den Worten vor: „Da heute Thanksgiving ist, haben wir Ihnen ein besonders schönes Geschenk mitgebracht. Hier ist etwas, wofür man wirklich dankbar sein kann." John Lennon tritt zum letzten Mal bei einem Konzert auf. Er singt im Madison Square Garden drei Stücke mit Elton John: *Whatever Gets You Through The Night*, *Lucy In The Sky With Diamonds* und *I Saw Her Standing There*. Nach dem Auftritt findet hinter der Bühne die Wiedervereinigung mit Yoko statt.

Annoncé par Elton John avec ces mots : « Comme c'est le jour de Thanksgiving, nous avons voulu vous offrir un cadeau spécial. Voici donc une bonne raison d'être reconnaissants... » Lennon donne ce qui sera son dernier concert en public, au Madison Square Garden, se joignant à son ami pour trois chansons : *Whatever Gets You Through The Night*, *Lucy In The Sky With Diamonds* et *I Saw Her Standing There*. Après le concert, en coulisses, il retrouve Yoko.

"The moment he walked out onstage, in a black suit and those round shades, he had the audience by its great, roaring throat, a noise like Liverpool supporters at a Cup Final as the team emerges from the tunnel. Even he was overwhelmed."

„In dem Augenblick, als er auf die Bühne trat, in einem schwarzen Anzug und mit einer runden Sonnenbrille, brach das Publikum in ein lautes Gebrüll aus, ein Geschrei wie von den Liverpool-Fans bei einem Endspiel, wenn die Mannschaft aus dem Tunnel auftaucht. Sogar er war überwältigt."

« À l'instant où il est entré sur scène, avec son costume noir et ses lunettes rondes, le public s'est mis à vociférer comme les supporters de Liverpool pendant une finale de Coupe d'Europe quand leur équipe sort du tunnel. Même lui a été submergé. »

MICHAEL WATTS, MELODY MAKER, DECEMBER 7, 1974

MONDAY, DECEMBER 16, 1974

After showing up at ABC-TV's "Monday Night Football" booth last week, during a game between the Los Angeles Rams and the Washington Redskins, talking with presenters Howard Cosell and Frank Gifford (Ronald Reagan is also in attendance and explains the rules of the game to him), Lennon guests on NBC-TV's "Today" show to promote his latest single *No. 9 Dream*. The **Daily Mail** in England reports that former President Nixon had ordered officials to 'harass Lennon and kick him out of America.'

John Lennon ließ sich eine Woche zuvor bei einem Footballspiel der Los Angeles Rams gegen die Washington Redskins auf der Tribüne von ABC „Monday Night Football" blicken und plauderte mit den Kommentatoren Howard Cosell und Frank Gifford (Ronald Reagan war ebenfalls anwesend und erklärte ihm die Spielregeln). An diesem Tag ist John Lennon in der NBC-Sendung „Today" zu Gast, um seine neue Single *No. 9 Dream* zu promoten. Die Zeitung **Daily Mail** in England berichtet, Expräsident Nixon habe seine Beamten aufgefordert, „Lennon zu schikanieren und aus Amerika herauszuschmeißen".

Après une participation la semaine précédente au commentaire d'un match entre les Rams de Los Angeles et les Redskins de Washington pour l'émission d'ABC « Monday Night Football », aux côtés des présentateurs Howard Cosell et Frank Gifford (Ronald Reagan se trouve aussi dans la cabine et lui explique les règles du jeu), Lennon est l'invité de « Today », sur NBC, pour faire la promotion de son dernier 45 tours, *No. 9 Dream*. Le **Daily Mail** anglais rapporte que l'ancien président Nixon a ordonné à ses fonctionnaires de « harceler Lennon et de le jeter hors d'Amérique ».

"The Government should let John Lennon live here in peace if he wishes. 'Tis the season ... Peace on earth!"

„Wenn John Lennon hier leben möchte, dann soll die Regierung ihn das bitte schön in Frieden tun lassen. Es ist Weihnachtszeit ... Friede auf Erden!"

« Le gouvernement devrait laisser John Lennon vivre ici en paix s'il le souhaite. « C'est Noël, après tout... Paix sur la Terre ! »

BILLBOARD, DECEMBER 28, 1974

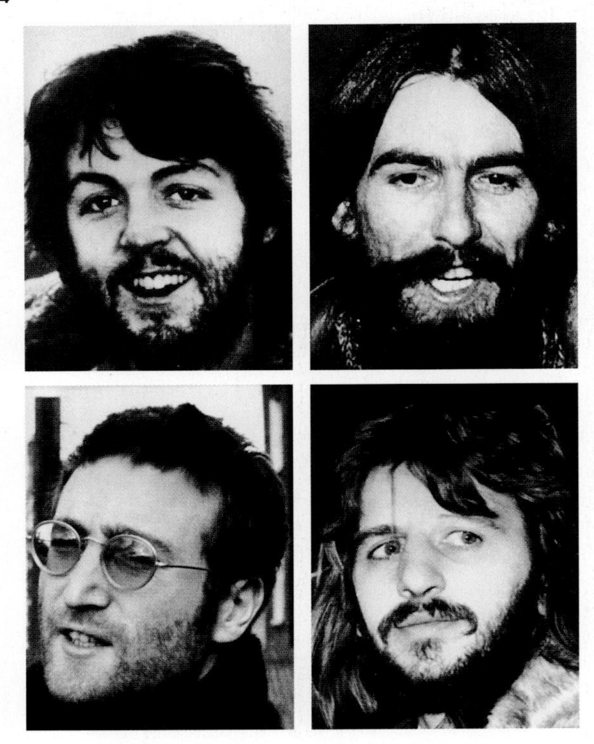

THURSDAY, JANUARY 9, 1975

The Beatles' partnership is finally dissolved at a private hearing before a high court judge, almost four years since Paul McCartney issued a writ seeking the end. The absolution of the partnership will not come into effect until April 9. (Lennon put his signature to the document at Disneyworld two weeks ago.)

Die Personengesellschaft The Beatles & Co. wird in einem nichtöffentlichen Verfahren vor einem Richter des High Court in London endlich aufgelöst, fast vier Jahre nachdem Paul McCartney mit seiner Klage deren Ende gesucht hatte. Die Auflösung der Personengesellschaft tritt jedoch erst am 9. April in Kraft. John Lennon hat seine Unterschrift zwei Wochen zuvor in Disneyworld unter das Dokument gesetzt.

Le partenariat juridique entre les Beatles est finalement dissout au cours d'une audience à huis clos, environ quatre ans après la demande déposée par Paul McCartney pour une régularisation de la situation. La dissolution n'entrera en vigueur que le 9 avril. (Lennon a signé le document deux semaines plus tôt, pendant un séjour à Disneyworld.)

SATURDAY, FEBRUARY 1, 1975

After a separation lasting 16 months, Lennon moves back into the couple's Dakota apartment. (In a March 6 statement, Lennon will say the separation was "not a success.")

Nach sechzehn Monaten Trennung zieht John Lennon wieder in die Wohnung im Dakota Building ein. (In einem Statement gibt John am 6. März bekannt, die Trennung sei „kein Erfolg" gewesen.)

Après une séparation de 16 mois, Lennon retourne s'installer au Dakota avec Yoko. (Le 6 mars, Lennon déclare que la séparation « n'a pas marché ».)

MONDAY, FEBRUARY 17, 1975

To counter the bootleg issue of ***Roots – John Lennon Sings The Great Rock & Roll Hits***, the official ***Rock 'n' Roll*** is rush-released in the United States. (Its British release will follow in four days time.)

Als Gegenmaßnahme gegen die Herausgabe des Bootlegs ***Roots – John Lennon Sings The Great Rock & Roll Hits*** wird die offizielle ***Rock 'n' Roll***-LP in den USA vorzeitig auf den Markt gebracht. (In Großbritannien wird sie vier Tage später veröffentlicht.)

Pour contrer l'album pirate ***Roots – John Lennon Sings The Great Rock & Roll Hits***, la sortie de l'album officiel ***Rock 'n' Roll*** est avancée en urgence aux États-Unis. (Il sort en Grande-Bretagne quatre jours plus tard.)

SATURDAY, MARCH 1, 1975

John and Yoko make their first public appearance since their reconciliation at the 17th annual Grammy Awards at the Uris Theatre in New York. John is joined by Paul Simon and Andy Williams to present the Grammy for Record of the Year. After the ceremony, John and Yoko attend a party, at which David Bowie is also present. Lennon and Bowie have just finished collaborating on a new song *Fame*, which will top the United States chart in September.

John und Yoko haben bei der 17. Verleihung der Grammy Awards im Uris Theater in New York ihren ersten gemeinsamen öffentlichen Auftritt, seit sie wieder zusammen sind. Gemeinsam mit Paul Simon und Andy Williams präsentiert John Lennon den Grammy für die beste LP des Jahres. Nach der Preisverleihung sind John und Yoko bei einer Party, an der auch David Bowie teilnimmt. John Lennon und David Bowie haben gerade ihre Zusammenarbeit an dem neuen Song *Fame* beendet, der es im September an die Spitze der US-Charts schafft.

John et Yoko font leur première apparition publique depuis leur réconciliation lors de la 17e cérémonie des Grammy Awards, à l'Uris Theatre de New York. John remet le G rammy du Disque de l'année avec Paul Simon et Andy Williams. John et Yoko se rendent ensuite à une soirée où est aussi invité David Bowie. Les deux hommes viennent de collaborer sur la chanson *Fame*, qui va occuper la première place des ventes aux États-Unis en septembre.

FRIDAY, JUNE 13, 1975

ABC-TV airs "Salute To Sir Lew—The Master Showman," in honor of the legendary television and film titan Sir Lew Grade. Lennon—making what will be his last TV appearance—performs *Slippin' And Slidin'*, *Stand By Me* and *Imagine*, backed by BOMF. Recorded at the Grand Ballroom of New York's Hilton Hotel on April 18, Lennon appears alongside Julie Andrews, Tom Jones, Peter Sellers and Dave Allen.

ABC-TV strahlt die Sendung „Salute To Sir Lew – The Master Showman" aus, ein Tribut an den legendären Film- und Fernsehproduzenten Lew Grade. Bei diesem letzten Fernsehauftritt spielt John Lennon *Slippin' And Slidin'*, *Stand By Me* und *Imagine* mit BOMF als Backingband. Die Sendung wurde am 18. April im Grand Ballroom des New Yorker Hilton Hotels aufgezeichnet, außer John Lennon treten auch Julie Andrews, Tom Jones, Peter Sellers und Dave Allen auf.

La chaîne ABC diffuse « Salute To Sir Lew – The Master Showman », en hommage à la légende de la télévision et du cinéma Sir Lew Grade. Lennon joue *Slippin' And Slidin'*, *Stand By Me* et *Imagine*, avec le groupe BOMF – ce sera son dernier passage télévisé. Pour cette émission enregistrée le 18 avril dans le grand salon de l'hôtel Hilton, à New York, Lennon partage l'affiche avec Julie Andrews, Tom Jones, Peter Sellers et Dave Allen.

THURSDAY, JUNE 19, 1975

Lennon files suit in Manhattan Federal Court against Government officials, including former Attorney General John Mitchell, charging that "deportation actions directed against (him) were improper."

John Lennon reicht eine Klage vor dem Bundesgericht Manhattan gegen Regierungsbeamte ein, u. a. gegen den ehemaligen Justizminister John Mitchell. Die Anklage lautet: „Das Abschiebungsverfahren gegen (ihn) sei unzulässig gewesen."

Lennon dépose une plainte devant la cour fédérale de Manhattan contre plusieurs représentants de gouvernement, notamment le procureur général John Mitchell, jugeant que les procédures d'expulsion lancées à son encontre sont sans fondement.

Elvis

TUESDAY, OCTOBER 7, 1975

The United States Court of Appeals for the Second Circuit, by a 2-1 decision, refers Lennon's case back to the INS, with a recommendation that the singer be allowed to stay in the United States. Chief Judge Irving R. Kaufman writes the decision for the majority. Two weeks ago in a brief announcement, Oswald K. Kramer, the INS's acting commissioner for North-eastern States, said the proceeding has been given "nonpriority: status," granting Lennon a temporary delay in deporting him on "humanitarian grounds" because Yoko was expecting.

Das Bundesberufungsgericht für den 2. Gerichtsbezirk verweist den Fall John Lennon in einer 2-zu-1-Entscheidung zurück an die Einwanderungsbehörde, mit der Empfehlung, dem Sänger eine dauerhafte Aufenthaltsgenehmigung zu erteilen. Der vorsitzende Richter Irving R. Kaufman schreibt die Mehrheitsbegründung. Zwei Wochen zuvor hat der Beauftragte der Einwanderungsbehörde für die nordöstlichen Staaten Oswald K. Kramer in einer kurzen Notiz mitgeteilt, das Verfahren habe jetzt den „Status: nicht mehr dringlich", womit John Lennons Abschiebung vorübergehend „aus humanitären Gründen" ausgesetzt werde, weil Yoko schwanger ist.

Par deux voix contre une, la cour d'appel des États-Unis pour le deuxième circuit renvoie le cas Lennon au département de l'Immigration, et recommande que l'artiste soit autorisé à rester aux États-Unis. Le juge Irving R. Kaufman rédige ces conclusions. Deux semaines plus tôt, Oswald K. Kramer, le commissaire de l'INS en charge des États du Nord-Est, annonçait laconiquement que le dossier Lennon était jugé « non-prioritaire » et que ses services avaient pour l'instant retardé la procédure d'expulsion à son encontre « pour des raisons humanitaires », parce que Yoko était enceinte.

"The courts will not condone selective deportation based upon secret political grounds ... Lennon's four-year battle to stay in our country is testimony to his faith in the American dream."

„Das Gericht wird eine selektive Abschiebung aus geheimen politischen Gründen nicht dulden ... Dass Lennon seit vier Jahren darum kämpft, in unserem Land bleiben zu dürfen, ist Zeugnis seines Glaubens an den amerikanischen Traum."

« Les tribunaux ne toléreront pas les expulsions sélectives motivées par des raisons politiques secrètes. [...] La bataille que mène Lennon depuis quatre ans pour rester dans notre pays témoigne de sa foi dans le rêve américain. »

CHIEF JUDGE IRVING R. KAUFMAN

"It's a great birthday gift from America for me, Yoko and the baby."

„Yoko und das Baby sind ein wunderbares Geburtstagsgeschenk Amerikas für mich."

« C'est un magnifique cadeau d'anniversaire que l'Amérique nous offre, à moi, à Yoko et au bébé ».

JOHN LENNON

seline

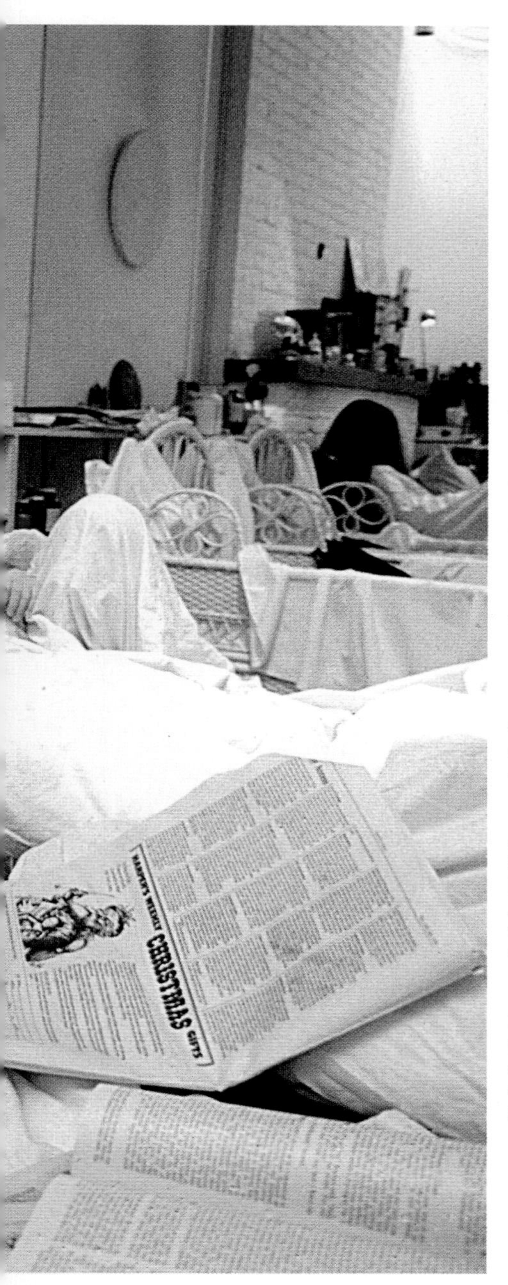

THURSDAY, OCTOBER 9, 1975

Sean Taro Ono Lennon is born in New York, automatically and ironically qualifying the infant as an American citizen. The birth of his only child by Ono has a profound effect on Lennon who will effectively retire for five years to become a househusband in his Manhattan apartment while Ono runs their business empire. Elton John becomes a proud godfather.

Sean Taro Ono Lennon kommt in New York auf die Welt, wodurch das Baby ironischerweise automatisch amerikanischer Staatsbürger wird. Die Geburt von John Lennons einzigem Kind mit Ono verändert sein Leben völlig, er zieht sich fünf Jahre lang aus der Öffentlichkeit zurück, wird Hausmann und Vater und bleibt zu Hause in der Wohnung in Manhattan, während Ono das Geschäftsimperium leitet. Elton John wird stolzer Patenonkel.

Sean Taro Ono Lennon naît à New York, ce qui fait automatiquement de lui (belle ironie) un citoyen américain. La naissance du seul enfant qu'il aura avec Yoko a un impact profond sur Lennon, qui décide de se retirer de la vie publique pour se consacrer à son rôle de père de famille dans son appartement de Manhattan, pendant qu'Ono gère l'empire. Elton John est fier d'être choisi comme parrain de l'enfant.

MONDAY, JANUARY 26, 1976

The Beatles' nine-year contract with EMI expires. McCartney re-signs with the company as a solo artist, while Harrison and Starr sign elsewhere. Lennon chooses neither option, and so is without a recording contract for the first time since 1962.

Der Neunjahresvertrag der Beatles mit EMI läuft aus. Paul McCartney unterzeichnet von neuem als Solokünstler beim selben Label, George Harrison und Ringo Starr schließen Verträge mit anderen Labeln. John Lennon nimmt keine der beiden Möglichkeiten wahr und ist zum ersten Mal seit 1962 ohne Plattenvertrag.

Le contrat de neuf ans signé entre les Beatles et EMI arrive à expiration. McCartney signe à nouveau avec la maison de disques en son nom propre, tandis que Harrison et Starr changent de distributeur. Lennon ne fait ni l'un ni l'autre, et se retrouve donc sans maison de disques pour la première fois depuis 1962.

SATURDAY, APRIL 24, 1976

Following several recent multi-million dollar offers by promoters for a Beatles reunion, Lorne Michaels—producer of NBC-TV's "Saturday Night Live"—announces on tonight's show that he has been authorized by NBC to offer the group $3,000. "All you have to do is sing three Beatle tunes—*She Loves You Yeah, Yeah, Yeah*—that's $1,000 right there. Like I said, this check is made out to the Beatles. You divide it up anyway you want. If you want to give Ringo less that's up to you." Unbeknownst to Michaels, Paul McCartney is spending the evening with Lennon at his Dakota apartment watching the show. (When George Harrison guests on "Saturday Night Live" in November, he will ask whether he can have the $3,000. Michaels replies "If it was up to me, you could have the money, but NBC wouldn't agree.")

Nachdem einige Promoter mehrere Millionen Dollar für eine Wiedervereinigung der Beatles angeboten haben, verkündet Lorne Michaels, Produzent der NBC-Kultsendung „Saturday Night Live", an diesem Abend in der Sendung, der NBC würde der Gruppe 3.000 Dollar für einen Auftritt zahlen. „Ihr braucht nichts weiter zu tun, als drei Beatles-Liedchen zu singen – *She Loves You Yeah, Yeah, Yeah*, Yeah – und schon habt ihr tausend Dollar verdient. Wie ich bereits sagte: Hier, der Scheck ist schon auf die Beatles ausgestellt. Ihr könnt euch das Geld teilen, wie ihr wollt. Wenn ihr Ringo weniger geben möchtet, ist das eure Sache." Was Michaels nicht ahnt: Paul McCartney sitzt zu diesem Zeitpunkt bei John in der Wohnung im Dakota Building und sieht sich mit ihm zusammen die Sendung an. (Als George Harrison im November bei „Saturday Night Live" zu Gast ist, fragt er, ob er die 3.000 Dollar haben kann. Michaels antwortet: „Von mir aus können Sie das Geld kriegen, aber der NBC würde nicht mitmachen. ")

Alors que les Beatles se sont vu proposer des contrats à plusieurs millions de dollars pour se réunir à nouveau sur scène, Lorne Michaels – le producteur de l'émission de la NBC « Saturday Night Live » – annonce qu'il a été autorisé par la chaîne à leur proposer un cachet de 3 000 dollars. « Tout ce que vous aurez à faire, c'est chanter trois titres des Beatles : *She Loves You Yeah, Yeah, Yeah*, et hop ! ça fait 1 000 dollars. Comme je l'ai dit, le chèque sera rédigé à l'ordre des Beatles. Vous vous le répartissez comme vous voulez. Si vous voulez donner moins à Ringo, c'est comme vous le sentez. » Michaels est loin de se douter que Paul McCartney est alors en train de passer la soirée avec Lennon au Dakota, et qu'ils regardent l'émission. (Quand George Harrison est invité au « Saturday Night Live » en novembre, il demande s'il peut avoir les 3 000 dollars, et Michaels lui répond : « Si ça ne dépendait que de moi, je vous donnerais l'argent, mais NBC ne serait pas d'accord. »)

TUESDAY, JULY 27, 1976

At a 90-minute hearing in the downtown New York offices of the Immigration and Naturalization Service, Judge Ira Fieldsteel approves Lennon's application for his green card (no: A17-597-321), allowing him permanent residence in the US. Gloria Swanson, Norman Mailer, Geraldo Rivera and sculptor Isamu Noguchi appear at the hearing as character witnesses. Celebrating the decision, John and Yoko retire to Serendipity's, an ice-cream parlor on the Upper East Side.

Nach einer 90-minütigen Anhörung auf dem Amt der Einwanderungsbehörde in Downtown New York bewilligt Richter Ira Fieldsteel John Lennons Antrag auf eine Green Card (Nr. A17-597-321), die dauerhafte Aufenthaltsgenehmigung in den USA. Gloria Swanson, Norman Mailer, Geraldo Rivera und Bildhauer Isamu Noguchi sind als Leumundszeugen bei der Anhörung anwesend. Zur Feier des Tages gehen John und Yoko hinterher in die Eisdiele Serendipity's in der Upper East Side.

Lors d'une audience de 90 minutes dans les bureaux de l'INS à Manhattan, le juge Ira Fieldsteel accorde à Lennon la carte verte (numéro : A17-597-321) qui l'autorise à demeurer aux États-Unis. Gloria Swanson, Norman Mailer, Geraldo Rivera et le scupteur Isamu Noguchi sont ses témoins de moralité. Pour fêter cette décision de justice, John et Yoko s'enferment au Serendipity's, un marchand de glace de l'Upper East Side.

"Now I'm going home to crack open a tea-bag and start looking at some travel catalogues."

„Jetzt gehe ich nach Hause, mache mir eine Tasse Tee und schaue mir ein paar Reiseprospekte an."

« Maintenant je vais rentrer chez moi me faire un bon thé et feuilleter des catalogues de voyage. »

JOHN LENNON

“I believe time wounds all heels.”

„Ich bin überzeugt, dass die Zeit alle Heiler verwundet.“

« Je pense que le temps blesse toutes les guérisons »

JOHN LENNON

“I think John Lennon is a great artist who has made an enormous contribution to popular culture. He is one of the great artists of the Western world. We lost T. S. Eliot to England, and only got Auden back.”

„Ich halte John Lennon für einen wichtigen Künstler, der einen enormen Beitrag zur Populärkultur geleistet hat. Er ist einer der größten Künstler der westlichen Welt. Wir haben schon T. S. Eliot an England verloren und nur Auden zurückbekommen.“

« Je pense que John Lennon est un grand artiste qui a immensément contribué à la culture populaire. Il est un des plus grands artistes d’Occident. Nous avons perdu T. S. Eliot au profit de l’Angleterre, et nous venons à peine de récupérer Auden. »

NORMAN MAILER

“We feel that good food is essential to physical well-being and we are anti-junk food.”

„Wir sind überzeugt, dass gutes Essen für das körperliche Wohlbefinden sehr wichtig ist, und treten gegen Junkfood ein.“

« Nous pensons qu’une nourriture de qualité est essentielle au bien-être physique, et nous sommes contre la “malbouffe”. »

GLORIA SWANSON

NEW YORK
CITY

WEDNESDAY, JANUARY 19, 1977

The Lennons attend President Jimmy Carter's Inauguration Ball at the Kennedy Center for the Performing Arts in Washington, DC where they mingle with Muhammad Ali, whom Lennon last encountered in 1964.

Die Lennons nehmen am Ball zur Amtseinführung von Präsident Jimmy Carter im Kennedy Center for the Performing Arts in Washington, D.C. teil, wo sie auch Muhammad Ali treffen, den John 1964 zum letzten Mal gesehen hat.

Les Lennon assistent à la soirée d'entrée en fonctions du président Jimmy Carter au Kennedy Center for the Performing Arts de Washington, où ils croisent Mohammed Ali, que Lennon n'a plus vu depuis 1964.

TUESDAY, OCTOBER 4, 1977

At a press conference at the Hotel Okura in Tokyo, Japan, Lennon reveals that his music career is on hold, so that he and Yoko can "be with our baby as much as we can until we feel we can take the time off to indulge ourselves in creating things outside the family." The Lennons have been in Japan since May.

Bei einer Pressekonferenz im Hotel Okura in Tokio sagt John Lennon, er habe eine Pause in seiner musikalische Karriere eingelegt, damit er und Yoko „so viel wie irgend möglich mit unserem Kind zusammen sein können, bis wir wieder das Gefühl haben, uns frei nehmen und den Luxus gönnen zu können, außerhalb der Familie kreativ zu sein". Die Lennons sind seit Mai in Japan.

Au cours d'une conférence de presse à l'hôtel Okura de Tokyo, au Japon, Lennon annonce qu'il met sa carrière musicale de côté pour que Yoko et lui puissent « passer autant de temps que possible avec [notre] bébé jusqu'à ce que [nous ayons] le sentiment que [nous pouvons] à nouveau prendre le temps de créer des choses en dehors de la famille ». Les Lennon se trouvent au Japon depuis mai.

SUNDAY, MAY 27, 1979

The Lennons take out full-page ads in the **New York Times** and the **Sunday Times**, headed "A Love Letter From John And Yoko—To People Who Ask Us What, When, And Why."

Die Lennons schalten ganzseitige Anzeigen in der **New York Times** und der **Sunday Times** mit der Überschrift: „Ein Liebesbrief von John und Yoko – An die Leute, die uns nach dem Was, Wann und Warum fragen."

Les Lennon achètent une pleine page dans le **New York Times** et le **Sunday Times**, intitulée « Une Lettre d'amour de John et Yoko – À ceux qui nous demandent quoi, quand et pourquoi ».

"Basically, I'm now a Zen pagan."

„Prinzipiell bin ich jetzt Heide und praktiziere Zen."

« Fondamentalement, je suis devenu un païen zen. »

JOHN LENNON, OCTOBER 4, 1977

1980

*"John had many faults which have been well aired,
but few people had the privilege to know what a warm and kind human being he was,
genuinely loving his fellow man. He was a true original. His zany sense of humor
could elevate the meanest of spirits. He will be sadly missed."*

*„John hatte viele Fehler, die hinlänglich bekannt sein dürften. Doch nur wenige Menschen hatten
das Vorrecht zu wissen, was für ein warmherziger, freundlicher Mensch er war, jemand, der seine
Mitmenschen aufrichtig geliebt hat. Er war ein echtes Original. Sein ausgeprägter Sinn für Humor
konnte selbst die finstersten Gemüter aufheitern. Er wird mir sehr fehlen."*

*« John a fait beaucoup d'erreurs, qui ont été largement médiatisées, mais peu de gens
ont eu le privilège de connaître l'être chaleureux et généreux qu'il était, son amour sincère
pour son prochain. C'était un véritable original. Son sens de l'humour loufoque
savait élever les esprits les plus vils. Il nous manquera cruellement. »*

GEORGE MARTIN

"I have been inundated with calls from investors wishing to buy my quarter share. The phone hasn't stopped ringing."

„Ich werde überschwemmt mit Anrufen von Investoren, die mein Viertel Anteil kaufen wollen. Das Telefon hört nicht auf zu klingeln."

« J'ai été inondé d'appels d'investisseurs qui souhaitaient acheter mes parts. Le téléphone n'a pas cessé de sonner. »

JOHN LENNON

WEDNESDAY, MAY 21, 1980

A press statement is released, announcing Lennon's plans to sever remaining links with the Beatles by selling his quarter share in Apple Corp Ltd.

In einer Pressemitteilung werden John Lennons Pläne bekannt gegeben, seine noch verbleibende Verbindung zu den Beatles aufzulösen und sein Viertel der Apple Corp. Ltd. zu verkaufen.

Lennon annonce dans un communiqué de presse son intention de couper ses derniers liens avec les Beatles en revendant ses parts dans l'Apple Corp Ltd.

WEDNESDAY, JUNE 4, 1980

After a brief vacation on his own in Cape Town, South Africa, Lennon travels to Bermuda (where he will be joined by Sean) on board the chartered 43-feet yacht, Megan-Jaye—fulfilling a lifelong ambition to sail. While there John begins writing new material while Yoko is doing likewise back in New York. Within three weeks they will have composed 25 songs.

Nach einem Kurzurlaub allein in Kapstadt segelt John Lennon an Bord der 13-Meter-Yacht Megan-Jaye nach Bermuda (wo Sean zu ihm stößt) und erfüllt sich damit einen lebenslangen Traum vom Segeln. In Bermuda angekommen, beginnt John neues Material zu schreiben, Yoko tut dasselbe zu Hause in New York. Sie komponieren 25 Stücke in drei Wochen.

Après de courtes vacances passées seul au Cap, en Afrique du Sud, Lennon part pour les Bermudes (où Sean le rejoint) sur le Megan-Jaye, le yacht de 13 mètres qu'il a loué ; il réalise ainsi un rêve de longue date. Pendant ce séjour, John recommence à écrire tandis que Yoko fait de même à New York. En trois semaines, ils composent 25 chansons.

MONDAY, AUGUST 4, 1980

After a musical hiatus which has lasted more than five years, John and Yoko begin recording at the Hit Factory in New York, with co-producer Jack Douglas. The sessions—which include today's takes of *(Just Like) Starting Over* and the Ono-penned *Kiss Kiss Kiss, I'm Moving On* and *Every Man Has A Woman Who Loves Him*—will yield 22 completed songs.

Nach über fünf Jahren Pause gehen John und Yoko wieder ins Studio, diesmal in die Hit Factory in New York, mit Jack Douglas als Koproduzent. Die Sessions – an diesem Tag werden Versionen von *(Just Like) Starting Over* und die von Ono geschriebenen Titel *Kiss Kiss Kiss, I'm Moving On* und *Every Man Has A Woman Who Loves Him* aufgenommen – ergeben am Ende 22 fertige Songs.

Après une pause musicale de plus de cinq ans, John et Yoko commencent à enregistrer à la Hit Factory de New York avec le coproducteur Jack Douglas. Les prises de *Kiss Kiss Kiss, I'm Moving On* et *Every Man Has A Woman Who Loves Him* (composés par Ono) et de *(Just Like) Starting Over* portent le nombre de chansons à 22.

MONDAY, SEPTEMBER 22, 1980

With all prior solo releases issued on the Beatles' Apple label, Lennon signs a five-year deal with Geffen Records, after David Geffen has offered to release the album without hearing any of the material.

Alle bisherigen Solo-Alben von John Lennon sind beim Apple-Label der Beatles erschienen, doch jetzt unterzeichnet er einen Fünfjahresvertrag mit Geffen Records, nachdem David Geffen angeboten hat, das Album zu veröffentlichen, ohne irgendetwas von dem Material gehört zu haben.

Tout son précédent répertoire en solo était la propriété du label Appel des Beatles, mais Lennon signe un contrat de cinq ans avec Geffen Records, David Geffen ayant accepté de sortir l'album sans même l'avoir écouté.

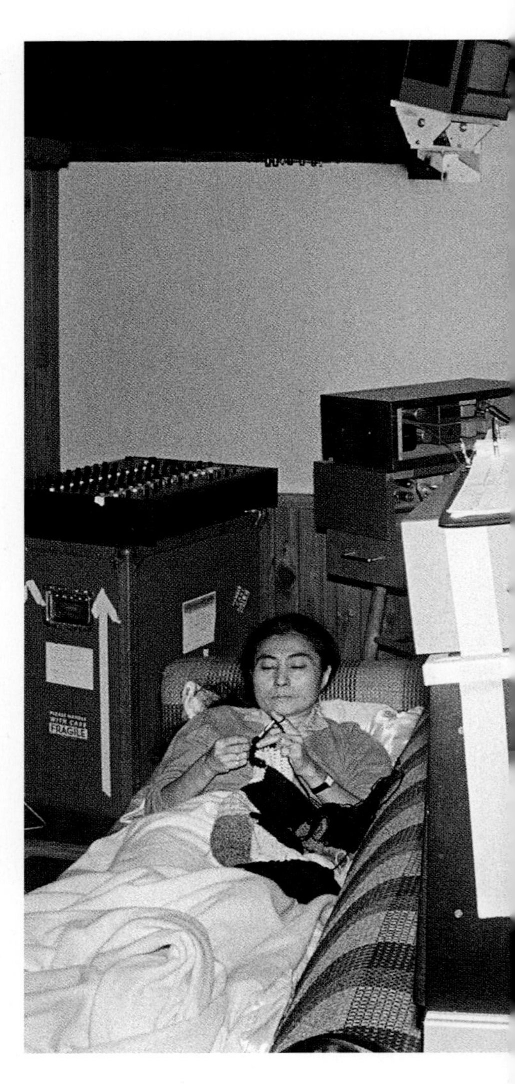

B

"The thing the sixties did was show us the possibility and responsibility that we all had. It wasn't the answer. It just gave us a glimpse of the possibility."

„Die Sechziger haben uns gezeigt, wie viele Möglichkeiten und Verantwortung wir alle haben. Die Antwort war es nicht. Sie haben uns nur einen kleinen Einblick in das gegeben, was möglich ist."

« Ce que les années 1960 nous ont montré, c'est les possibilités et les responsabilités que nous avons tous. Ce n'était pas la solution. Elles ne nous ont donné qu'un aperçu de nos possibilités. »

JOHN LENNON, RKO RADIO INTERVIEW, DECEMBER 8, 1980

THURSDAY, OCTOBER 9, 1980

A skywriter flies over Manhattan writing "Happy Birthday John & Sean—Love Yoko" nine times in the sky. It is John's 40th and Sean's 5th.

Ein Himmelsschreiber fliegt über Manhattan und schreibt neunmal „Happy Birthday John & Sean – Love Yoko" in den Himmel. Es ist Johns 40. und Seans 5. Geburtstag.

Un avion dessine neuf fois dans le ciel de Manhattan le message « Happy Birthday, John & Sean – Love, Yoko ». John fête ses 40 ans et Sean ses 5 ans.

SATURDAY, NOVEMBER 17, 1980

Credited to John Lennon and Yoko Ono, ***Double Fantasy*** is released to mostly positive reviews, as Lennon makes a full return to the limelight. An optimistic set underpinned by themes of love and family, it features session musicians Hugh McCracken and Earl Slick (guitars), Tony Levin (bass), George Small (keyboards) and Andy Newmark (drums).

Double Fantasy von John Lennon und Yoko Ono als Komponisten wird von größtenteils positiven Kritiken begrüßt, und John kehrt ins Rampenlicht zurück. Die optimistische LP mit den Themen Liebe und Familie entstand mit den Studiomusikern Hugh McCracken und Earl Slick (Gitarre), Tony Levin (Bass), George Small (Keyboard) und Andy Newmark (Drums).

Composé et écrit par John Lennon et Yoko Ono, ***Double Fantasy*** est globalement bien accueilli par la critique et Lennon retourne sous le feu des projecteurs. Les musiciens de studio Hugh McCracken et Earl Slick (guitares), Tony Levin (basse), George Small (claviers) et Andy Newmark (batterie) l'accompagnent pour cet opus optimiste où les thèmes de l'amour et de la famille dominent.

"You make your own dream ... Don't expect Jimmy Carter or Ronald Reagan or John Lennon or Yoko Ono or Bob Dylan or Jesus Christ to come and do it for you. You have to do it yourself. That's what the great masters and mistresses have been saying ever since time began."

„Jeder ist für seinen Traum selbst verantwortlich ... Man darf nicht erwarten, dass Jimmy Carter oder Ronald Reagan oder John Lennon oder Yoko Ono oder Bob Dylan oder Jesus Christus kommt und einem das abnimmt. Das muss man schon selbst tun. Das haben die großen Meister und Meisterinnen seit Beginn aller Zeiten gesagt."

« C'est à vous de réaliser vos rêves. [...] Ne comptez pas sur Jimmy Carter, Ronald Reagan, John Lennon, Yoko Ono, Bob Dylan ou Jésus Christ pour qu'ils le fassent à votre place. C'est à vous de le faire. C'est ce que répètent tous les grands maîtres, hommes et femmes, depuis l'aube des temps. »

JOHN LENNON, PLAYBOY

MONDAY, DECEMBER 8, 1980

Following a four-hour session working on Yoko's *Walking On Thin Ice*, Lennon and Ono leave the Record Plant studio at 10:30 p.m. They enter the West 72nd Street entrance of the Dakota building and Lennon turns around when he hears a voice say, "Mr. Lennon." He is shot four times by 25-year-old Mark David Chapman, before struggling up six stairs to inside the alcove of the guard area, where he collapses at approximately 10:50 p.m. Two bullets have hit him in the back, piercing his lung and passing through his chest. Two more hit him in the shoulder, one shattering his left shoulder bone, the other ricocheting inside his chest severing his aorta. A fifth bullet misses. The police receive a five-word report: "Man shot. One West 72nd." Officers Peter Cullen and Steve Spiro—a couple of blocks away—are first on the scene, where they find Lennon bleeding profusely. Officers Tony Palma and Herb Frauenberger arrive next, and place Lennon in the back seat of Officers James Moran and William Gamble's patrol car, who drive to the Roosevelt Hospital on West 59th Street. Despite the efforts of a team of seven medics, he is pronounced dead from a massive loss of blood at 11:07 p.m. Lennon is 40 years old. He will be transported in a body bag from the hospital morgue to the Frank E. Campbell Funeral Chapel at Madison and 81st Street. On Wednesday, his body will be cremated at the Ferncliff Mortuary in Hartsdale, thirty miles outside of New York.

Nach einer vierstündigen Session, bei der sie an Yokos *Walking On Thin Ice* gearbeitet haben, verlassen John und Yoko das Record-Plant-Studio um 22:30 Uhr. Sie wollen gerade das Dakota Building am Eingang an der West 72nd Street betreten, als John eine Stimme sagen hört: „Mr. Lennon" und sich umdreht. Der 25-jährige Mark David Chapman gibt vier Schüsse auf ihn ab, bevor John sich die sechs Stufen zum Alkoven des Portiers hochschleppen kann, wo er um ca. 22:50 Uhr zusammenbricht. Zwei Schüsse haben ihn in den Rücken getroffen, seine Lunge durchbohrt und sind an der Brust wieder ausgetreten. Zwei weitere haben ihn in die Schulter getroffen, einer hat seine linke Schulterpfanne zerschmettert, ein anderer Querschläger geht in die Brust und durchtrennt die Aorta. Ein fünfter Schuss verfehlt ihn. Die Polizei erhält eine Fünf-Wort-Meldung: „Mann angeschossen. West 72nd eins." Die Streifenbeamten Peter Cullen und Steve Spiro sind nur wenige Blocks entfernt und treffen als Erste am Tatort ein, wo sie den stark blutenden John Lennon vorfinden. Als Nächstes treffen die Polizisten Tony Palma und Herb Frauenberger ein, die John auf dem Rücksitz des Streifenwagens der Polizisten James Moran und William Gamble ins Roosevelt Hospital an der West 59th Street transportieren. Trotz aller Bemühungen eines Teams von sieben Medizinern wird er um 23:07 Uhr für tot durch zu starken Blutverlust erklärt. John Lennon ist 40 Jahre alt. Er wird in einem Leichensack aus der Leichenhalle des Krankenhauses zur Frank E. Campbell Funeral Chapel Ecke Madison und 81st Street gebracht. Am Mittwoch wird sein Leichnam im Ferncliff Mortuary in Hartsdale, fünfzig Kilometer außerhalb von New York, eingeäschert.

Après quatre heures de travail sur la chanson de Yoko *Walking On Thin Ice*, Lennon et Ono quittent les studios Record Plant à 22h30. Ils s'approchent de l'entrée du Dakota sur la 72ᵉ rue Ouest lorsque Lennon se retourne en entendant quelqu'un dire « Mr. Lennon ». Mark David Chapman, 25 ans, tire sur lui à cinq reprises. Lennon réussit à monter les six marches du perron et à entrer dans l'alcôve du gardien, où il s'effondre à environ 22h50. Deux balles l'ont atteint dans le dos, transperçant son poumon et sa poitrine. Deux autres l'ont touché à l'épaule, l'une brisant son omoplate gauche, l'autre ricochant dans sa poitrine jusqu'à heurter l'aorte. La police reçoit un appel bref : « Un homme abattu. N° 1 de la 72ᵉ rue ». Les agents Peter Cullen et Steve Spiro – qui se trouvent à deux rues de là – sont les premiers sur les lieux, où ils découvrent Lennon baignant dans son sang. Les agents Tony Palma et Herb Frauenberger arrivent peu après et placent Lennon à l'arrière de la voiture de patrouille des agents James Moran et William Gamble, qui le conduisent à l'hôpital Roosevelt, sur la 59ᵉ rue Ouest. Malgré les efforts déployés par une équipe de sept médecins, son décès, provoqué par une perte de sang massive, est prononcé à 23h07. Lennon avait 40 ans. Il est transporté dans un sac mortuaire de la morgue de l'hôpital à la chapelle funéraire Frank E. Campbell, sur Madison et la 81ᵉ rue. Le mercredi, son corps est incinéré chez Ferncliff Mortuary, à Hartsdale, à une quarantaine de kilomètres de New York.

"Love and peace are eternal."

„Liebe und Frieden sind ewig."

« La paix et l'amour sont éternels. »

JOHN LENNON

"John Lennon held out hope. He imagined, and however quietistic he became he never lost that utopian identification."

„John Lennon hat die Hoffnung nie aufgegeben. Er hatte einen Traum, und diese Identifikation mit einer Utopie hat er nie verloren, auch wenn er ruhiger geworden ist."

« John Lennon gardait espoir. Il avait un rêve, et aussi paisible qu'il soit devenu, il n'a jamais perdu cette identité utopiste. »

ROBERT CHRISTGAU, VILLAGE VOICE, DECEMBER, 1980

© Christie's

TUESDAY, DECEMBER 9, 1980

The night following Lennon's death, Bruce Springsteen & the E. Street Band perform at the Spectrum in Philadelphia. Before they begin their performance Springsteen says, "I'd just like to say one thing, I appreciate it and it's a hard night to come out and play tonight when so much has been lost. The first record that I ever learned was a record called *Twist And Shout*, and if it wasn't for John Lennon, we'd all be in some place very different tonight. It's an unreasonable world and you have to live with a lot of things that are just unlivable, and it's a hard thing to come out and play but there's just nothing else you can do."

Am Abend nach John Lennons Tod treten Bruce Springsteen und die E. Street Band im Spectrum in Philadelphia auf. Vor dem Konzert sagt Bruce Springsteen: „Eine Sache will ich noch sagen. Ich weiß es zu schätzen und es ist schwer, an solch einem Abend rauszugehen und zu spielen, an dem man so viel verloren hat. Die erste Schallplatte, die ich kannte, war eine Scheibe, die *Twist And Shout* hieß, und wenn es John Lennon nicht gegeben hätte, wäre keiner von uns da, wo er jetzt ist. Es ist eine sinnlose Welt und man muss mit so vielen Dingen leben, die man nicht aushalten kann, und es ist schwer, jetzt hier zu spielen, aber wir können ja nichts anderes tun."

Au lendemain de la mort de Lennon, Bruce Springsteen & the E. Street Band se produisent au Spectrum de Philadelphie. Avant de commencer le concert, Springsteen déclare : « Je voudrais juste dire une chose... merci... parce que c'est difficile de venir jouer devant vous ce soir, quand nous avons tant perdu. Le premier morceau que j'ai jamais appris s'appelait *Twist And Shout*, et si John Lennon n'avait pas existé, nous serions tous dans un endroit bien différent ce soir. Ce monde est insensé et nous sommes obligés de supporter beaucoup de choses qui sont simplement insupportables. C'est difficile de jouer pour vous ce soir, mais il n'y a rien d'autre que nous puissions faire. »

SUNDAY, DECEMBER 14, 1980

With fans the world over still coming to terms with Lennon's death, Yoko Ono requests that all those who wish to remember him should observe ten minutes silence from 2:00 p.m. Eastern Standard Time. With hundreds still keeping a vigil outside the Dakota building, approximately 100,000 people gather in Central Park with another 30,000 converging outside St. George's Hall on Lime Street in Liverpool.

Fans auf der ganzen Welt können John Lennons Tod immer noch nicht fassen. Yoko Ono fordert alle Trauernden auf, zu seiner Erinnerung um 14 Uhr Ostküstenzeit zehn Schweigeminuten einzulegen. Hunderte halten nach wie vor eine Mahnwache vor dem Dakota Building, an die 100.000 Menschen versammeln sich im Central Park und weitere 30.000 kommen vor der St. George's Hall an der Lime Street in Liverpool zusammen.

Alors que dans le monde entier les fans restent sous le choc de la mort de Lennon, Yoko Ono demande à tous ceux qui souhaitent lui rendre hommage d'observer dix minutes de silence à partir de 14h00, heure de la côte Est. Des centaines de personnes se massent devant le Dakota, environ 100 000 fans se réunissent dans Central Park et 30 000 à Liverpool, devant le St. George's Hall de Lime Street.

SATURDAY, DECEMBER 27, 1980

With the irony-laced *(Just Like) Starting Over* already in its second week at No. 1 in the United Kingdom, (holding off the reissued *Happy Xmas (War Is Over)* at No. 2), it now tops the United States chart. Meanwhile ***Double Fantasy*** begins an eight-week run at No. 1, during which time it will also find pole position in the United Kingdom.

Das ironische Stück *(Just Like) Starting Over* ist bereits in der zweiten Woche auf Platz eins der britischen Charts (das neu herausgebrachte *Happy Xmas (War Is Over)* belegt den zweiten Platz) und schafft es jetzt auch an die Spitze der US-Charts. ***Double Fantasy*** hält sich ab diesem Tag acht Wochen lang auf dem ersten Platz in den USA und schafft es auch in England bis ganz nach oben.

Alors que le cruellement ironique *(Just Like) Starting Over* entame sa deuxième semaine au sommet des charts britanniques – devant la réédition de *Happy Xmas (War Is Over)* – il arrive en première place des ventes aux États-Unis. ***Double Fantasy*** y reste huit semaines en première place, et l'atteint aussi au Royaume-Uni.

"John was a great man. His death is a bitter, cruel blow—I really loved the guy. He was one of the best. He will be sadly missed by the whole world. John will be remembered for his contribution to art, music and world peace. I can't tell you how much it hurts to lose him."

„John war ein ganz besonderer Mensch. Sein Tod ist ein bitterer, grausamer Schlag – ich habe ihn wirklich sehr gern gehabt. Er war einer der Besten. Die ganze Welt wird ihn fürchterlich vermissen. John wird für seine Leistungen in der Kunst, Musik und für den Weltfrieden unvergesslich bleiben. Ich kann nicht mit Worten ausdrücken, wie weh es tut, ihn verloren zu haben."

« John était un grand homme. Sa mort est une épreuve amère, cruelle – j'aimais vraiment ce type. Il faisait partie des meilleurs. Il manquera cruellement au monde entier. John restera dans les mémoires pour sa contribution à l'art, à la musique et à la paix dans le monde. Je ne peux pas vous dire à quel point le perdre fait mal. »

PAUL MCCARTNEY

"After all we went through together I had and still have great love and respect for him. To rob someone of life is the ultimate crime. It is an outrage that people can take other people's lives when they obviously haven't got their own lives in order."

„Nach allem, was wir zusammen durchgemacht haben, hatte und habe ich noch immer große Zuneigung und Respekt für ihn. Jemanden seines Lebens zu berauben, ist das größte Verbrechen. Es ist ein Skandal, wenn jemand einem anderen Menschen das Leben nehmen kann, bloß weil derjenige sein eigenes Leben offensichtlich nicht in Ordnung bringen kann."

« Après tout ce que nous avons vécu ensemble, j'ai toujours eu et j'aurai toujours un amour sincère et un profond respect pour lui. Dépouiller quelqu'un de sa vie est le pire crime que l'on puisse commettre. Il est scandaleux que des gens puissent prendre la vie d'autres gens alors qu'à l'évidence ils ne maîtrisent pas leur propre vie. »

GEORGE HARRISON

"John Lennon helped create the music and the mood of our time. His spirit, the spirit of the Beatles—brash and earnest, ironic and idealistic all at once—became the spirit of the whole generation. His work as an artist and musician was far from over ... It is especially poignant that John Lennon has died by violence, though he had long campaigned for peace."

„John Lennon hat dazu beigetragen, die Musik und Stimmung unserer Zeit zu schaffen. Sein Geist, der Geist der Beatles – frech und aufrecht, ironisch und idealistisch zugleich – wurde zum Geist einer ganzen Generation. Seine Arbeit als Künstler und Musiker war noch lange nicht beendet ... Es ist besonders schmerzlich, dass John Lennons Leben ein gewaltsames Ende fand, obwohl er sich so lange für den Frieden eingesetzt hat."

« John Lennon a participé à la création de la musique et de l'esprit de notre temps. Son esprit, celui des Beatles – effronté et sincère, ironique et idéaliste tout à la fois – est devenu l'esprit de toute une génération. Son œuvre d'artiste et de musicien était loin d'être achevée. [...] Il est particulièrement poignant que John Lennon ait succombé à la violence, lui qui avait tant milité pour la paix. »

PRESIDENT JIMMY CARTER

"John loved and prayed for the human race. Please do the same for him."

„John liebte die ganze Menschheit und betete für sie. Bitte tut das Gleiche für ihn."

« John aimait la race humaine et priait pour elle. S'il vous plaît, faites la même chose pour lui. »

YOKO ONO

POSTSCRIPT

POSTSKRIPTUM

POST-SCRIPTUM

IMA

WEDNESDAY, OCTOBER 9, 1985

Yoko and Sean attend the opening ceremony of "Strawberry Fields", an area in Central Park—opposite the Dakota apartments—designated by New York city council in March 1981 to honor the slain legend. With Ono having contributed $500,000 to redesign and renovate the area, its eastern section, designed by landscape architect Bruce Kelly, is called the "Garden of Peace." 150 nations will eventually contribute plants to the garden.

Yoko und Sean nehmen an der Einweihungsfeier der „Strawberry Fields" teil, einem Stück Central Park gegenüber dem Dakota Building. Das Parkgelände wurde von der New Yorker Stadtverwaltung im März 1981 dem Andenken an die ermordete Poplegende geweiht. Yoko hat eine halbe Million Dollar zur Umgestaltung und Verschönerung des Geländes gestiftet, dessen östlicher, von dem Landschaftsarchitekten Bruce Kelly gestalteter Abschnitt „Garten des Friedens" heißt. 150 Nationen steuern Pflanzen zu dem Garten bei.

Yoko et Sean assistent à l'inauguration de « Strawberry Fields », une zone aménagée dans Central Park, face au Dakota, et commandée par la municipalité en mars 1981 pour honorer l'icône assassinée. Yoko Ono a fait don de 500 000 dollars pour en rénover la partie orientale, redessinée par le paysagiste Bruce Kelly et baptisée le « Jardin de la Paix ». Quelque 150 pays enverront des arbres pour qu'ils y soient plantés.

TUESDAY, OCTOBER 9, 1990

Imagine is played simultaneously in 130 countries to commemorate what would have been Lennon's 50th birthday. A live worldwide broadcast is beamed from the United Nations, consisting of a short introduction by Marcela Pérez de Cuéllar, wife of the UN Secretary-General, and a taped message of Lennon followed by the playing of his seminal signature peace anthem.

Imagine wird zur Feier von John Lennons 50. Geburtstag in 130 Ländern zeitgleich gespielt. Aus dem Hauptsitz der Vereinten Nationen wird eine Live-Sendung weltweit übertragen, die aus einer kurzen Einführung von Marcela Pérez de Cuéllar, der Frau des UN-Generalsekretärs, und einer aufgezeichneten Botschaft von John Lennon besteht, gefolgt von seiner unsterblichen Friedenshymne.

Imagine est joué simultanément dans 130 pays pour commémorer ce qui aurait été le 50e anniversaire de Lennon. Émise en mondovision depuis le siège des Nations Unies, la cérémonie est lancée par un bref discours de l'épouse du secrétaire général des Nations unies, Marcela Pérez de Cuéllar ; un message enregistré de Lennon est ensuite diffusé avant que retentisse son fameux hymne.

"The thing you must remember is that I'm the number one John Lennon fan. I love him to this day and I always did love him. All these people assembled to thank you for everything that you mean to all of us. Tonight you're in the Rock and Roll Hall of Fame. God bless you."

„Sie dürfen nie vergessen, dass ich der größte John-Lennon-Fan bin. Ich habe ihn immer geliebt und liebe ihn bis zum heutigen Tag. All diese Menschen hier haben sich versammelt, um dir für all das zu danken, was du uns bedeutest. Heute Abend bist du in der Rock and Roll Hall of Fame. Gott segne dich."

« Ce dont vous devez vous souvenir, c'est que je suis le plus grand fan de John Lennon. Je l'aime encore à ce jour et je l'ai toujours aimé. Tous ces gens sont rassemblés ici pour te remercier de tout ce que tu représentes pour nous. Ce soir, tu entres au Rock and Roll Hall of Fame. Que Dieu te bénisse. »

PAUL MCCARTNEY

WEDNESDAY, JANUARY 19, 1994

At an especially poignant awards ceremony in New York, John Lennon is posthumously inducted by Paul McCartney into the Rock and Roll Hall of Fame at the ninth annual dinner held at the Waldorf Astoria Hotel.

Mit einer besonders bewegenden Zeremonie führt Paul McCartney John Lennon beim neunten Jahresdinner im New Yorker Waldorf-Astoria Hotel posthum in die Rock and Roll Hall of Fame ein.

Au cours d'une cérémonie particulièrement émouvante à New York, Paul McCartney intronise John Lennon au Rock and Roll Hall of Fame à titre posthume, lors du neuvième dîner organisé à l'hôtel Waldorf Astoria.

SUNDAY, NOVEMBER 24, 2002

John Lennon is named the eighth Greatest Briton in the BBC's list of 100 Greatest Britons, one place behind Her Royal Majesty, Queen Elizabeth I and 11 places higher than Paul McCartney.

John Lennon erreicht auf der BBC-Liste der 100 bedeutendsten Briten den 8. Platz. Er ist damit der achtwichtigste Brite aller Zeiten, einen Platz hinter Ihrer Majestät, Königin Elisabeth I. und elf Plätze vor Paul McCartney.

John Lennon arrive huitième de la liste des « 100 personnalités britanniques les plus importantes » établie par la BBC, juste derrière la Reine Elizabeth I et 11 places devant Paul McCartney.

3

ESSENTIAL RECORDINGS

DIE WICHTIGSTEN ALBEN

PRINCIPAUX ENREGISTREMENTS

LIVE PEACE IN TORONTO (1969)

1 Blue Suede Shoes **2** Money (That's What I Want) **3** Dizzy Miss Lizzy **4** Yer Blues **5** Cold Turkey **6** Give Peace A Chance **7** Don't Worry, Kyoko (Mummy's Only Looking For Her Hand In The Snow **8** John, John (Let's Hope For Peace)

PLASTIC ONO BAND (1970)

1 Mother **2** Hold On **3** I Found Out **4** Working Class Hero **5** Isolation **6** Remember **7** Love **8** Well Well Well **9** Look At Me **10** God **11** My Mummy's Dead **12** Power To The People **13** Do The Oz

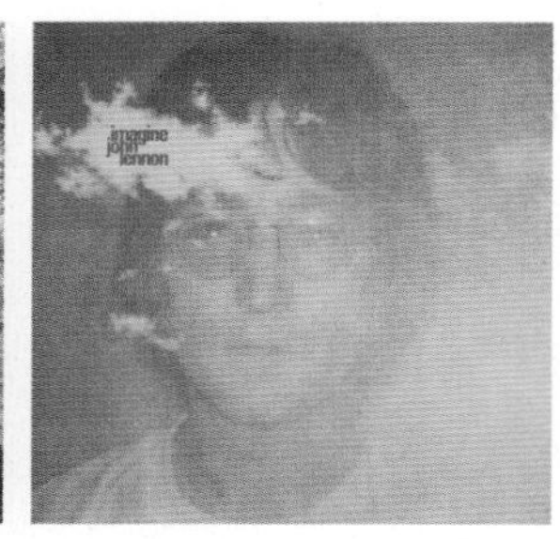

IMAGINE (1971)

1 Imagine **2** Crippled Inside **3** Jealous Guy **4** It's So Hard **5** I Don't Want To Be A Soldier **6** Give Me Some Truth **7** Oh My Love **8** How Do You Sleep? **9** How? **10** Oh Yoko!

SOME TIME IN NEW YORK CITY/LIVE JAM (1972)

1 Woman Is The Nigger Of The World **2** Sisters, O Sisters **3** Attica State **4** Born In A Prison **5** New York City **6** Sunday Bloody Sunday **7** The Luck Of The Irish **8** John Sinclair **9** Angela **10** We're All Water **11** Cold Turkey (live) **12** Don't Worry, Kyoko (live) **13** Well (Baby, Please Don't Go) (live) **14** Jamrag (live) **15** Scumbag **16** Aü (live)

MIND GAMES (1973)

1 Mind Games **2** Tight A$ **3** Aisumasen (I'm Sorry) **4** One Day (At A Time) **5** Bring On The Lucie (Freda Peeple) **6** Nutopian International Anthem **7** Intuition **8** Out The Blue **9** Only People **10** I Know (I Know) **11** You Are Here **12** Meat City

WALLS AND BRIDGES (1974)

1 Going Down On Love **2** Whatever Gets You Through The Night **3** Old Dirt Road **4** What You Got **5** Bless You **6** Scared **7** #9 Dream **8** Surprise, Surprise (Sweet Bird Of Paradox) **9** Steel And Glass **10** Beef Jerky **11** Nobody Loves You (When You're Down And Out) **12** Ya Ya

ROCK 'N' ROLL (1975)

1 Be-Bop-A-Lula **2** Stand By Me **3** Medley: Rip It Up/Ready Teddy **4** You Can't Catch Me **5** Ain't That A Shame **6** Do You Want To Dance? **7** Sweet Little Sixteen **8** Slippin' And Slidin' **9** Peggy Sue **10** Medley: Bring It On Home To Me/Send Me Some Lovin' **11** Bony Maronie **12** Ya Ya **13** Just Because

SHAVED FISH (1975)

1 Medley: Give Peace A Chance/Cold Turkey **2** Instant Karma! **3** Power To The People **4** Mother **5** Woman Is The Nigger Of The World **6** Imagine **7** Whatever Gets You Through The Night **8** Mind Games **9** #9 Dream **10** Medley: Happy Xmas (War Is Over)/Give Peace A Chance (Reprise)

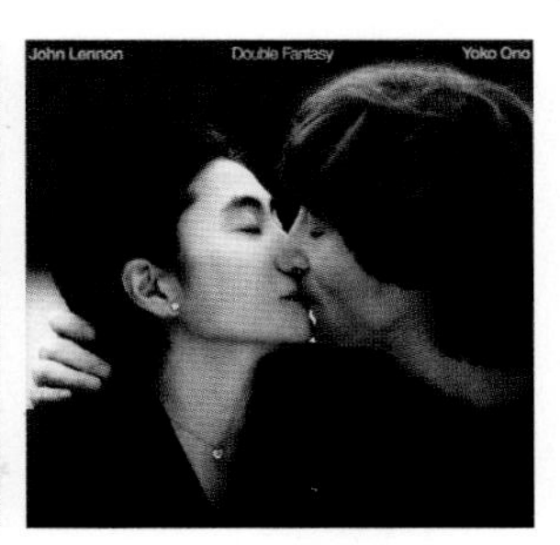

DOUBLE FANTASY (1980)

1 (Just Like) Starting Over **2** Kiss Kiss Kiss **3** Cleanup Time **4** Give Me Something **5** I'm Losing You **6** I'm Moving On **7** Beautiful Boy (Darling Boy) **8** Watching The Wheels **9** I'm Your Angel **10** Woman **11** Beautiful Boys **12** Dear Yoko **13** Every Man Has A Woman Who Loves Him **14** Hard Times Are Over

MILK AND HONEY (1984)

1 I'm Stepping Out **2** Sleepless Night **3** I Don't Wanna Face It **4** Don't Be Scared **5** Nobody Told Me **6** O'Sanity **7** Borrowed Time **8** Your Hands **9** (Forgive Me) My Little Flower Princess **10** Let Me Count The Ways **11** Grow Old With Me **12** You're The One

MENLOVE AVE (1986)

1 Here We Go Again **2** Rock And Roll People **3** Angel Baby **4** Since My Baby Left Me **5** To Know Her Is To Love Her **6** Steel And Glass **7** Scared **8** Old Dirt Road **9** Nobody Loves You (When You're Down And Out) **10** Bless You

IMAGINE (SOUNDTRACK) (1988)

1 Real Love **2** Twist And Shout **3** Help! **4** In My Life **5** Strawberry Fields Forever **6** A Day In The Life **7** Revolution **8** The Ballad Of John And Yoko **9** Julia **10** Don't Let Me Down **11** Give Peace A Chance **12** How? **13** Imagine (rehearsal) **14** God **15** Mother **16** Stand By Me **17** Jealous Guy **18** Woman **19** Beautiful Boy (Darling Boy) **20** (Just Like) Starting Over **21** Imagine

4

AWARDS & CHART HISTORY

AUSZEICHNUNGEN & CHARTPLATZIERUNGEN

RÉCOMPENSES ET HISTORIQUE DES VENTES

UNITED STATES CERTIFICATIONS
UNITED STATES SINGLES

Instant Karma – Gold / ***(Just Like) Starting Over*** – Gold / ***Woman*** – Gold

UNITED STATES ALBUMS

Plastic Ono Band – Gold / ***Mind Games*** – Gold / ***Walls And Bridges*** – Gold / ***Milk And Honey*** – Gold / ***Double Fantasy*** – 3 times Platinum / ***Imagine – Music From The Motion Picture*** – Gold / ***Imagine*** – 2 times Platinum / ***Rock 'n' Roll*** – Gold / ***Shaved Fish*** – Platinum / ***The John Lennon Anthology*** – Gold / ***The John Lennon Collection*** – 3 times Platinum / ***Live in New York City*** – Gold / ***Lennon Legend – The Very Best Of John Lennon*** – Platinum

UNITED KINGDOM CERTIFICATIONS
UNITED KINGDOM SINGLES

Imagine – Platinum / ***(Just Like) Starting Over*** – Gold / ***Woman*** – Silver

UNITED KINGDOM ALBUMS

Mind Games – Gold / ***Walls And Bridges*** – Silver / ***Shaved Fish*** – Gold / ***Rock 'n' Roll*** – Gold / ***Double Fantasy*** – Platinum / ***Milk And Honey*** – Gold / ***The John Lennon Collection*** – 3 times Platinum / ***Imagine – Music From The Motion Picture*** – Gold / ***Lennon Legend – The Very Best Of John Lennon*** – 2 times Platinum / ***Legend*** – Platinum / ***Working Class Hero – The Definitive Lennon*** – Gold

GRAMMY AWARDS

Album of the Year – ***Double Fantasy*** 1981

GRAMMY HALL OF FAME

Imagine **–** 1999

MISCELLANEOUS AWARDS

Outstanding Contribution to British Music, Ivor Novello Awards, 1981 / Outstanding Contribution to Music, BRIT Awards, 1982 / Songwriters Hall of Fame, 1987 / Star on Hollywood Walk of Fame, 1988 / Inducted into the Rock and Roll Hall of Fame (as a Beatle), 1989 / Inducted into the Rock and Roll Hall of Fame, 1994 / Nordoff-Robbins Music Therapy Center Silver Clef Award, 1997 / No. 8, Greatest Briton, BBC Television, 2002 / No. 38, The Immortals – The Fifty Greatest Artists of All Time, **Rolling Stone**, 2004 / No. 5, 100 Greatest Singers of All Time, **Rolling Stone**, 2008

CHART HISTORY

US CHART SINGLES

Week of Entry	*Highest Position*	*Wks*	*Title*	*Catalog Number*
62 *(July 26, 1969)*	14 *(September 6, 1969)*	9	***Give Peace A Chance***	Apple 1809
86 *(November 15, 1969)*	30 *(January 17, 1970)*	12	***Cold Turkey***	Apple 1813
65 *(February 28, 1970)*	3 *(March 28, 1970)*	13	***Instant Karma (We All Shine On)***	Apple 1818
87 *(January 9, 1971)*	43 *(January 30, 1971)*	6	***Mother***	Apple 1827
73 *(April 3, 1971)*	11 *(May 1, 1971)*	9	***Power To The People***	Apple 1830
20 *(October 23, 1971)*	3 *(November 13, 1971)*	9	***Imagine***	Apple 1840
76 *(November 10, 1973)*	18 *(December 29, 1973)*	13	***Mind Games***	Apple 1868
53 *(September 28, 1974)*	1 *(November 16, 1974)*	15	***Whatever Gets You x Thru The Night***	Apple 1874
68 *(December 21, 1974)*	9 *(February 22, 1975)*	12	***#9 Dream***	Apple 1878
78 *(March 15, 1975)*	20 *(April 26, 1975)*	9	***Stand By Me***	Apple 1881
38 *(November 1, 1980)*	1 *(December 27, 1980)*	22	***Starting Over***	Geffen 49604
36 *(January 17, 1981)*	2 *(March 21, 1981)*	20	***Woman***	Geffen 49644
77 *(March 28, 1981)*	10 *(May 23, 1981)*	17	***Watching The Wheels***	Geffen 49695
82 *(March 31, 1984)*	55 *(April 21, 1984)*	6	***I'm Steppin' Out***	Polydor 821107-7
36 *(January 21, 1984)*	5 *(March 3, 1984)*	14	***Nobody Told Me***	Polydor 817254-7
84 *(October 15, 1988)*	80 *(October 22, 1988)*	4	***Jealous Guy***	Capitol 44230

US CHART ALBUMS

Week of Entry	*Highest Position*	*Wks*	*Title*	*Catalog Number*
158 *(February 8, 1969)*	124 *(March 22, 1969)*	8	***Unfinished Music No. 1 : Two Virgins***	Apple 5001
197 *(June 28, 1969)*	174 *(August 2, 1969)*	8	***Unfinished Music No. 2 : Life With The Lions***	Zapple 3357
182 *(December 13, 1969)*	178 *(December 27, 1969)*	3	***Wedding Album***	Apple 3361
136 *(January 10, 1970)*	10 *(February 7, 1970)*	32	***Live Peace In Toronto 1969***	Apple 3362
14 *(December 26, 1970)*	6 *(January 30, 1971)*	27	***John Lennon/Plastic Ono Band****	Apple 3372
163 *(September 18, 1971)*	1 *(October 30, 1971)*	45	***Imagine***	Apple 3379
190 *(July 1, 1972)*	48 (August 12, 1972)	17	***Some Time In New York City****	Apple 3392
16 *(November 24, 1973)*	9 *(December 8, 1973)*	31	***Mind Games***	Apple 3414
72 *(October 12, 1974)*	1 *(November 16, 1974)*	35	***Walls And Bridges***	Apple 3416
47 *(March 8, 1975)*	6 *(April 19, 1975)*	15	***Rock 'N' Roll***	Apple 3419
97 *(November 8, 1975)*	12 *(December 13, 1975)*	14	***Shaved Fish***	Apple 3421
25 *(December 6, 1980)*	1 *(December 27, 1980)*	74	***Double Fantasy***	Geffen 2001
45 *(December 4, 1982)*	33 *(January 8, 1983)*	16	***The John Lennon Collection***	Geffen 2023
185 *(January 14, 1984)*	94 *(February 25, 1984)*	12	***Heartplay*****	Polydor 817238
39 *(February 11, 1984)*	11 *(March 10, 1984)*	19	***Milk And Honey*****	Polydor 817160
77 *(March 22, 1986)*	41 *(April 5, 1986)*	11	***Live In New York City***	Capitol 12451
193 *(November 22, 1986)*	127 *(November 29, 1986)*	4	***Menlove Ave.***	Capitol 12533
144 *(October 22, 1988)*	31 *(November 19, 1988)*	18	***Imagine : John Lennon***	Capitol 90803
76 *(March 14, 1998)*	65 *(March 21, 1998)*	9	***Lennon Legend - The Very Best Of John Lennon***	Parlophone 21954
99 *(November 21, 1998)*	99 *(November 21, 1998)*	2	***John Lennon Anthology***	Capitol 30614
31 *(November 20, 2004)*	31 *(November 20, 2004)*	6	***Acoustic***	Capitol 74428
135 *(October 22, 2005)*	135 *(October 22, 2005)*	3	***Working Class Hero - The Definitive Lennon***	Capitol 40391

* with the Plastic Ono Band / ** with Yoko Ono

UK CHART SINGLES

Week of Entry	Highest Position	Wks	Title	Catalog Number
21 *(July 12, 1969)*	2 *(July 26, 1969)*	18	**Give Peace A Chance**	Apple APPLE 13
38 *(November 1, 1969)*	14 *(November 15, 1969)*	8	**Cold Turkey**	Apple APPLES 1001
7 *(February 21, 1970)*	5 *(February 28, 1970)*	9	**Instant Karma!**	Apple APPLES 1003
12 *(March 20, 1971)*	7 *(April 3, 1971)*	9	**Power To The People**	Apple R 5892
23 *(December 9, 1972)*	2 *(January 10, 1981)*	26	**Happy Xmas (War Is Over)**	Apple R 5970
39 *(November 24, 1973)*	26 *(December 8, 1973)*	7	**Mind Games**	Apple R 5994
41 *(October 19, 1974)*	36 *(November 2, 1974)*	4	**Whatever Gets You Thru' The Night**	Apple R 5998
49 *(February 8, 1975)*	23 *(March 8, 1975)*	8	**#9 Dream**	Apple R 6003
48 *(May 3, 1975)*	30 *(May 24, 1975)*	7	**Stand By Me**	Apple R 6005
43 *(November 1, 1975)*	1 *(January 10, 1981)*	24	**Imagine**	Apple R 6009
30 *(November 8, 1980)*	1 *(December 20, 1980)*	15	**(Just Like) Starting Over**	Geffen K 79186
3 *(January 24, 1981)*	1 *(February 7, 1981)*	11	**Woman**	Geffen K 79195
47 *(March 21, 1981)*	40 *(March 28, 1981)*	4	**I Saw Her Standing There**	DJM DJS 10965
54 *(April 4, 1981)*	30 *(April 18, 1981)*	6	**Watching The Wheels**	Geffen K 79207
56 *(November 20, 1982)*	41 *(December 4, 1982)*	7	**Love**	Parlophone R 6059
11 *(January 21, 1984)*	6 *(January 28, 1984)*	6	**Nobody Told Me**	Ono Music/Polydor POSP 700
51 *(March 17, 1984)*	32 *(April 7, 1984)*	6	**Borrowed Time**	Polydor POSP 701
65 *(November 30, 1985)*	65 *(November 30, 1985)*	2	**Jealous Guy**	Parlophone R 6117
66 *(December 10, 1988)*	45 *(December 17, 1988)*	5	**Imagine/Jealous Guy/ Happy Xmas (War Is Over)**	Parlophone R 6199
3 *(December 25, 1999)*	3 *(December 25, 1999)*	13	**Imagine**	Parlophone CDR 6534
33 *(December 20, 2003)*	33 *(December 20, 2003)*	3	**Happy Xmas (War Is Over)**	Parlophone CDR 6627
60 *(December 15, 2007)*	40 *(December 22, 2007)*	3	**Happy Xmas (War Is Over)**	Parlophone 29800675

UK CHART ALBUMS

Week of Entry	Highest Position	Wks	Title	Catalog Number
1 *(October 30, 1971)*	1 *(October 30, 1971)*	102	**Imagine**	Apple PAS 10004
18 *(January 16, 1971)*	11 *(January 23, 1971)*	11	**John Lennon/Plastic Ono Band***	Apple PCS 7124
11 *(October 14, 1972)*	11 *(October 14, 1972)*	6	**Sometime In New York City***	Apple PCSP 716
44 *(December 8, 1973)*	13 *(December 15, 1973)*	12	**Mind Games**	Apple PCS 7165
14 *(October 19, 1974)*	6 *(October 26, 1974)*	10	**Walls And Bridges**	Apple PCTC 253
19 *(March 8, 1975)*	6 *(March 15, 1975)*	28	**Rock 'N' Roll**	Apple PCS 7169
53 *(November 8, 1975)*	8 *(December 6, 1975)*	29	**Shaved Fish**	Apple PCS 7173
27 *(November 22, 1980)*	1 *(February 7, 1981)*	36	**Double Fantasy****	Geffen K99131
20 *(November 20, 1982)*	1 *(December 4, 1982)*	43	**The John Lennon Collection**	Parlophone EMTV 37
3 *(February 4, 1984)*	3 *(February 4, 1984)*	13	**Milk And Honey****	Polydor POLH 5
55 *(March 8, 1986)*	55 *(March 8, 1986)*	3	**John Lennon Live In New York City**	Parlophone PCS 7031
69 *(October 22, 1988)*	64 *(November 5, 1988)*	6	**Imagine (Original Soundtrack)**	Parlophone PCSP 722
4 *(November 8, 1997)*	4 *(November 8, 1997)*	45	**Lennon Legend -**	Parlophone 8219542
62 *(November 14, 1998)*	62 *(November 14, 1998)*	1	**Anthology**	Capitol 8306142
11 *(October 15, 2005)*	11 *(October 15, 2005)*	10	**Working Class Hero - The Definitive John Lennon**	Parlophone 3400802

BIBLIOGRAPHY

Badman, Keith: *The Beatles – After The Break-up 1970-2000 – A Day By Day Diary.* Omnibus Press, 1999.
Coleman, Ray: *John Ono Lennon.* Sidgwick & Jackson, 1984.
Crampton, Luke & Dafydd Rees: *Rock & Roll – Year By Year.* Dorling Kindersley, 2003.
Henke, James: *Lennon Legend – An Illustrated Life Of John Lennon.* Chronicle Books, 2003.
Kane, Larry: *Lennon Revealed.* Running Press, 2005.
Lewisohn, Mark: *The Complete Beatles Chronicles.* Pyramid Books, 1992.
Norman, Philip: *John Lennon – The Life.* HarperCollins, 2008.
Pang, May: *Instamatic Karma – Photographs of John Lennon.* St. Martin's Press, 2008.
Partridge, Elizabeth: *John Lennon – All I Want Is The Truth.* Viking, 2005.
Periodicals/Newspapers: Billboard, Christian Science Monitor, Crawdaddy, Creem, Disc & Music Echo, Downbeat, Goldmine, Hi Fidelity/Musical America, Jazz & Pop, Life, Look, Los Angeles Times, Melody Maker, Music & Musicians, New Musical Express, New York Times, Newsweek, Record Business, Record Mirror, Rolling Stone, Time, The Times, Variety, Village Voice, Washington Post.

IMPRINT

Hohenzollernring 53, D-50 672 Köln
www.taschen.com

Editor: Luke Crampton & Dafydd Rees/ Original Media/www.original-media.net
Picture Research: Dafydd Rees & Wellesley Marsh
Editorial Coordination: Florian Kobler and Mischa Gayring, Cologne
Production Coordination: Nadia Najm and Horst Neuzner, Cologne
Design: Sense/Net, Andy Disl and Birgit Eichwede, Cologne
German Translation: Anke Burger, Berlin
French Translation: Alice Pétillot, Paris
Multilingual Production: www.arnaudbriand.com, Paris

Printed in China
ISBN 978-3-8365-1758-4

ACKNOWLEDGEMENTS
Larry Andrew, Mark Antman, Joan Athey, Mitch Blank, Adam Chandler, Cecilia de Querol, Sarah Field, David Ford Jr., Sara Fox, Tony Gale, Ralf Gartner, Bob Gruen, James Henke, Elizabeth Kerr, David Leaf, Rob Lifson, Matthew Lutts, Glen Marks, Joe Medina, Trish Murphy, Yoko Ono, Brian Pekny, Michelle Press, Elsa Ravazzolo, David Scripps, Jochen Sperber, Allan Tannenbaum, Kelly Wong.